Psychic Phenomena and Religion

PSYCHIC PHENOMENA AND RELIGION:

ESP, Prayer, Healing, Survival

by
H. RICHARD NEFF

THE WESTMINSTER PRESS
Philadelphia

ISBN 0-664-24931-0
LIBRARY OF CONGRESS CATALOG CARD No. 70-158122

Book Design by
Dorothy Alden Smith

Published by The Westminster Press
®
Philadelphia, Pennsylvania

PRINTED IN THE UNITED STATES OF AMERICA

CONTENTS

PREFACE

Psychic phenomena is a controversial topic. Part of the controversy involves the way people have characterized evidence presented in support of psychic events. Visions and voices are not considered adequate foundations for theories to support prayer, healing, and personal survival. Another part of the controversy involves the view we have of our world. We have been conditioned to believe that the raw data of human experiences from which we learn about our world can be received only through our five senses. The very name of one aspect of parapsychology—extrasensory perception (ESP)—challenges this generally accepted presupposition. The view that all human phenomena must fit the presently accepted categories of the physical and human sciences stands as a barrier to serious consideration of psychic events.

Especially since this is a controversial topic, I want to say concerning myself, first, that I claim no unusual psychic gifts. I am not a clairvoyant, a healer, a medium, or a spiritualist. Nor have I had a wealth of personal experiences in this broad area. To satisfy my own curiosity, I have repeated some of the experiments others have conducted; but I have not designed any new experiments. I am a clergyman, an ordained United Presbyterian minister, who has served three congregations in the past thirteen years. Through these years of pastoral experience I have developed an interest in some of the unusual phenomena that persons have reported to me—spiritual healings that have occurred, visions of a deceased relative, premonitions of coming events, and dreams that have foretold the future. At the same time I have observed the contemporary movement of theology away from the spiritual or supernatural dimension in human experience. At a certain point in my own pilgrimage three years ago I decided to investigate the area of psychic experience to see whether it is a part of reality or a psychological aberration. I have been engaged in an educational program at San Francisco Theological Seminary, so I made this project a part of my work there.

Throughout the study that is reported in this book I have attempted to maintain an attitude of honest and open-minded skepticism. I have sought to avoid prejudgment either in favor of or in opposition to the reality of psychic phenomena. I have tried to take seriously the evidence in this area and then probe and test to determine what this evidence indicates. I hope I have neither closed my mind nor been uncritical.

It is with some degree of apprehension that I present this material to the reading public. Investigation in the area of parapsychology is not well developed. There may be some new findings uncovered in the next few years that will force the revision of one or several of the conclusions I reach in this book. Yet I suppose, in this era of rapidly expanding knowledge, everyone must hold his conclusions in any field with some degree of tentativeness. But I believe my apprehension really is the fear of being misunderstood. This subject, I have discovered, is charged with emotion. To attempt to say anything on such a topic is to invite misunderstanding. I can only plead with my readers to note carefully what I say and not to read into my comments more than I have written.

I have discovered in the process of studying this topic that there is a rapidly growing interest in psychic phenomena. The first time I went to the local library to get some books in this field, many of the ones I wanted were not there. When I questioned the librarian, he told me that books on parapsychology are continually in circulation. I have learned, too, that some of the societies organized to study psychic phenomena are experiencing tremendous growth. Popular magazines are highlighting articles relating to occult practices, and scholarly journals are reporting parapsychology experiments. In the church, interest in spiritual healing is increasing, and a new wave of curiosity over neo-Pentecostalism is developing. Even people who are not directly participating in these religious and occult activities are curious about them and sometimes puzzled by them. Thus, this book is an attempt to help people who are interested in psychic phenomena to develop a critical perspective that will assist them in making informed judgments on what is believable and what is not.

Numerous people have helped me in this project. I want to mention two in particular. My wife, Trudy, has shared in my experience of investigating psychic phenomena and has successfully played the role of the skeptic to keep me from reaching unwarranted conclusions. The adviser for my academic project, Dr. Henry B. Adams, who is the executive director of the Academy of Parish Clergy, has made valuable criticisms of the work reported in this book. I appreciate what they and others have done to help me in this project. Although these persons have contributed significantly to this book, the responsibility for what appears on these pages is mine. I wish to express appreciation, also, to Mrs. Lon Alford, who typed the manuscript.

H.R.N.

1

A NEW POINT OF VIEW

There was a day when people believed the earth was flat. We can understand why; they believed what they saw. They looked around the countryside, and it looked flat. When they traveled to the next town, they went up on hills and down into valleys, but they appeared to be traveling on a level plane. It seemed ridiculous to them to consider that the earth might be anything but flat. The sensory evidence they accumulated from the land on which they lived became the basis for the interpretation they formed—the earth is flat.

Then someone, perhaps a person who lived near the sea, made a new observation. He noticed that when a ship sailed out from the shore, the hull first slipped below the horizon, and slowly the sails followed until the entire ship was below the line of sight. Could it be, our anonymous observer asked, that the earth is round like a ball? The first men who made such a ridiculous suggestion were greeted with scornful laughter. Slowly their number grew, however, and some of them had the courage to test their new conviction. Columbus and others sailed west to reach India, where others had gone by traveling east.

But it was not until Magellan's crew sailed west and came back to the point from which they had started in the east that the skeptics were convinced. Here was positive proof that the earth is round. People then shifted their belief from the flat-earth theory to the round-earth theory, because new and conclusive sensory evidence demonstrated that the earth is round.

For four centuries now, most people have believed that the earth is round. However, when the astronauts from the early manned Apollo missions returned with those beautiful pictures taken from several hundred miles above the earth, a curious news release appeared in a paper I read. According to the news article, these pictures, which clearly displayed the curvature of the earth, were shown to the president of the Flat Earth Society, a small group of people who hold unswervingly to the conviction that the earth is flat. When he saw the pictures, he is reported to have said, "It's amazing how round it looks to the untutored eye."

There are several observations we can make from these illustrations. The first is that we usually form our view of the world from the observations we and other people make. Our ideas and opinions grow from our perception of the world in which we live. So, for example, a theory of evolution, which is constructed on the observation of similar physical structures in animal life, becomes believable for us when we notice what Darwin and others have pointed out. The second observation we can make is that when new evidence is offered to us and we accept it, we must alter or discard the old theories concerning our world and form new theories that include the new possibilities. New evidence produces new convictions and beliefs. At the present time, we have no solid evidence that there are living things elsewhere in our universe. But if, on a flight into space, some living cells were collected, or if some evidence suggesting living forms in other areas of the universe came to us, we would have to construct a theory to include the possibility of life beyond the earth. A third observation to be made from the previous illustrative material is that some people may cling tenaciously to old theories that new evidence has indicated are in error. For various reasons they close their minds to this new evidence and accept a theory that cannot be supported. So a person may believe that the earth is flat or the moon is made of green cheese despite the conclusive evidence that contradicts his convictions.

We live in an era when ideas, opinions, beliefs, and convictions are in a state of flux. Change is continually taking place in our world, and new evidence that contradicts old opinions requires the formation of new theories. We have become more accustomed to new ideas, new opinions, and new styles of life than previous generations were.

One type of new evidence that calls for revised theories concerning both life and communication comes from psychic phenomena, the subject matter of this book. Theories that include the possibility of extrasensory perception may be constructed on evidence from human experience. Some events that are paranormal occur in human experience; that is, they are beyond the generally accepted categories of sensory experience. These events indicate that it is possible for information to be transmitted from one mind to another without the use of any of the recognized sensory organs; the medium of communication is extrasensory. Such evidence calls for new theories: that extrasensory perception may occur under certain conditions and that information we do not perceive in a normal way influences our thought processes. These theories, some critics point out, have not been demonstrated conclusively. An act comparable to Magellan's sailing around the world has not been accomplished for psychic phenomena. But some evidence is there, and it should not be ignored. Many people have closed their minds to this evidence. They may consider this field to be the province of quacks and freaks who engage in dangerous speculation, or they may not want their world view disturbed. However, I think that although some of the evidence for ESP, personal survival, prayer, and spiritual healing, and some of the practitioners associated with these fields are highly suspicious, there is some evidence that is worth serious consideration.

Before proceeding to that evidence, I want to define some basic terms. I have mentioned psychic phenomena; what is this? A dictionary definition of psychic is "not physical; lying outside the known physical processes." This is an accurate description of the phenomena that are called psychic—extrasensory perception, telepathy, clairvoyance, precognition, visions, healing forces, mediumship, and other paranormal matters. These phenomena are located well below the level of consciousness in the human psyche, or mind. This alone makes them very difficult to describe and define with precision. They imply, too, some perceptual activity beyond sensory perception. A shorthand designation for psychic phenomena that occurs occasionally in this book is the Greek letter *psi*. This is a general symbol which includes all the subject matter in this field. Some other terms that you will encounter on these pages use the prefix *para*, which sometimes means "beyond." Paranormal describes an event that is beyond what present scientific categories define as normal. The study of these events is para-psychology, which is literally "beyond psychology."

Some people feel that the material included in psychic phenomena belongs to the field of psychology. Certainly the psychologist studies dreams, hallucinations, and in-tuitions, but he describes them in terms of known sensory and mental categories. The parapsychologist, on the other hand, believes that these psychic phenomena do not fit into the current categories and theories used to describe human thought and perception. The traditional position of psychology, for example, is that all dreams are sym-bolic representations of the concerns and thoughts in our subconscious minds. The position of parapsychology is that some dreams may contain information coming from sources outside a person and transmitted to his mind by extrasensory means. Here, then, is the difference: the psychologist attempts to fit all unusual psychic phenom-ena into the current categories of his discipline, whereas the parapsychologist searches for new categories and theories beyond current psychological theory to describe these events.

Parapsychology is the application of scientific method to the study of psychic phenomena. Some people describe parapsychology as a pseudoscience or, at best, a quasi-science. The study of parapsychology is in infant stages, and the results of these studies are inconclusive and im-precise when compared with the findings in the physical sciences. Nevertheless, parapsychology does what other scientific disciplines do; that is, it applies scientific methods to the study of phenomena in the world and it forms theories from the data gathered. Parapsychology has achieved some degree of approval in scientific circles with the recent acceptance of the Parapsychological Association into the American Association for the Advancement of Science. Parapsychology experiments that provide data concerning ESP, prayer, personal survival, and spiritual healing will be described in this book. Some of these experiments have been conducted in a laboratory with instruments and methods that measure precisely the data. Others have been observations and studies made on the "field." They have been done by careful and dedicated researchers in parapsychology.

There are at least two other forms in addition to scientific experiments in which psychic phenomena appear in our world. One is in religious ritual. Prayer and spiritual healing that produce paranormal results have some part in religious ritual. Spiritualism, too, is a religious practice that uses some of the principles and practices of mediumship. The other form that psychic phenomena takes in human experience is occult practices—mediumship, palmistry, fortune-telling, astrology, ouija boards, table tipping, etc. Some readers may perceive a gradation in the order in which these have been presented—scientific experiments, religious ritual, and occult practices. My bias is showing, but I would quickly point out that I do not consider all parapsychology experiments good or all occult practices bad. In parapsychology there are some excellent experiments and some poor ones. Among religious rituals there are some good methods and some poor ones. Even in the world of the occult, where there are so many opportunities for fraud, there are some honest and careful practitioners. No one of these three expressions of psychic phenomena is all good or all bad. Nevertheless, one must recognize that the difficulty parapsychologists experience in gaining respectability comes largely from widespread prejudice against the imprecise and, in some cases, deliberately fraudulent practices of occult devotees. Persons who use the mystery of psychic events to gain some kind of advantage over gullible, naïve people cast suspicion on the whole field. However, no field should be judged exclusively by the practice of its "lunatic fringe."

The important question is where the dividing line is between the authentic and the spurious in this field. It is a very difficult line to find. The central purpose I have in writing this book is to indicate what appears to me to be authentic. A good friend of mine read a magazine article I wrote on the topic, "The Church and Psychic Phenomena." In a letter he subsequently sent me he commented on his experience in this field. "I'm not really skeptical," he said; "I just run into too many blind corners." I am writing this book mainly for the many people who have some interest in these matters but who have hit too many blind corners in their search for truth. In addition, I write with the hope that some persons who have closed their minds on this topic because they feel that it is unscientific will open them again when they learn of the responsible scientific experiments that are being conducted by parapsychologists. And I hope that some persons who have uncritically accepted claims concerning mediumship, healing, or some other aspect of this field will reevaluate their conclusions.

I believe that parapsychology is a legitimate scientific pursuit. The field is in its infant stages, and there is still much that is not known. Nevertheless, significant discoveries have been made. I recognize, however, that some persons make extravagant claims about psychic phenomena. I have tried to avoid this. I have attempted to be very careful in drawing my conclusions so that I do not assume any more than the evidence supports. You will find in the book much indefinite language—statements that evidence "points toward" or "indicates" rather than "proves." You will find, also, that two or more conclusions may be drawn from some evidence. I have purposely written this way because in practically all instances the final verdict is not in; in many instances the final verdict is not even in sight. When I do indicate a personal preference for one possible conclusion over another, I try to make clear that this is a personal judgment and not a judgment that has behind it wide scholarly support. You may find the indefinite language frustrating, but this is the only way I can honestly present this material.

Although this book contains descriptions of experiments, it is not meant to be a technical work. For the most part, nontechnical language is used. The technical works that report the experimental procedures and results are in the notes for those who are interested in studying this subject more intensively.

The psychic dimension of human phenomena has not been adequately explored; in many cases it has not even been taken seriously. My conviction is that some of these phenomena are real and that they should be the subject of careful, thorough research. There is more here than meets the eye. I would encourage you to become with me an open-minded skeptic, willing to accept a new point of view where the evidence warrants it. Let us begin to "test the spirits."

2

EXTRASENSORY PERCEPTION

The normal channels a person uses to receive information from the world and the people around him are his five sense organs. Before a person dresses in the morning, he may look out of his bedroom window to see what kind of day it is. He may listen to the morning weather report to hear what kind of day it will be. If it looks as if it is raining though he cannot be certain, he may even put his hand out of the window to feel if raindrops are falling. As he dresses, the smell of bacon frying tells him something about the breakfast his wife is preparing. When he sits down at the breakfast table, he begins to taste what has been prepared. In this way he uses his five senses to learn what is going on in his world.

Communication between persons is normally sensory. I hope that I am communicating with you; information from my mind is conveyed to your mind through words I have written that you see with your eyes. If we were in the same room, we could communicate with words that are spoken. Your ears would be the means of hearing not only words but also tones and inflections that would reveal my enthusiasm or lack of it for this subject. By observing my posture, my gestures, and my facial expressions you would pick up additional sensory cues that would reveal my attitude toward you and toward the subject of our conversation.

Sensory cues come through the other senses as well. A handshake may tell you tactually something about another person or something about his impression of you. Olfactory cues in communication, highlighted in those televised advertisements for deodorants, perfumes, and dentifrices, can be very important. Even taste can be a means of communication when a woman carefully prepares a favorite dish for her husband. In many ways each day we perceive things from our world and from the people around us by sensory means.

But is the communication we receive from our world limited to what we perceive through our five senses? If you have a strong impression that someone you love is in grave danger and you subsequently learn that the impression of danger coincided with an actual event in which the life of your loved one was endangered, is it possible that that information was communicated by extrasensory means? Events similar to this have occurred with sufficient frequency to encourage some people to explore this possibility.

ESP IN LIFE

Extrasensory perception is one of those terms which carry their meaning in their own name. It is what it says: the perception of some fact or event by a means that is not part of the recognized perceptual operation of any known sensory apparatus. An event occurs and a person somehow knows that it has occurred, but he has not received any part of this information through any of the five sense organs: eyes, ears, nose, taste buds, or tactile nerve endings. It should be pointed out that this definition describes a phenomenon and reveals nothing about how the phenomenon occurs. As a matter of fact, when researchers discover how ESP occurs, the definition will have to be altered, for then a new sensory apparatus will be identified, and such perception will no longer be extrasensory.

Extrasensory perception is a natural phenomenon that is associated with living organisms. It was first observed in nature, and then the investigation of ESP through experimentation was begun in the laboratory. Dr. Louisa E. Rhine, wife of the pioneer ESP experimenter J. B. Rhine, and his co-worker, has collected over ten thousand reports of spontaneous ESP which persons have experienced and reported to her. She has included numerous examples from her files in her two books *Hidden Channels of the Mind* [1] and *ESP in Life and Lab.* [2] Rather than repeat on these pages what is found in these sources, I will record some occurrences of which I have personal knowledge, which seem to be best explained by ESP. These personal accounts may not be so dramatic and vivid as many that Dr. Rhine reports, but they illustrate the fact that such phenomena are not totally uncommon experiences.

A sixteen-year-old girl visited her mother, who was hospitalized in a city one hundred miles from their home. Her mother had not been feeling well and had entered the hospital for tests and possible surgery. There was no reason for this young lady to believe that her mother was dangerously ill, but as she walked down the corridor of the hospital after that visit, she received the strong impression that her mother would never leave the hospital. An operation the next week revealed that her mother had cancer, which would be terminal, but still there was no reason to believe that her mother would not be able to come home, for she had months, perhaps more than a year, of life expectancy. However, one week after the surgery she suffered a pulmonary embolism and died. The young lady in this situation is now my wife.

A boy in college was practicing with a church choir. At the time, he knew an uncle was hospitalized and was very ill. In the middle of one of the numbers of Mozart's "Requiem," he suddenly sensed that his uncle had died. When he arrived home, he learned that, in fact, this is what had happened. This was a personal experience of mine.

A minister had been contacted by a pastoral nominating committee to explore the possibility of his becoming pastor of their church. Six of the nine committee members came one Sunday to observe him leading in worship and to talk with him after the service. The next Sunday the remaining three were to come; then he and his wife were to visit the prospective church to talk with the entire committee there. Everything went according to schedule with one exception. On the second Sunday only two committee members came to the service, leaving one woman on the committee as the only one of the nine who had not heard him preach. After these initial contacts, several weeks went by with no further communication between the minister and the committee members. One Sunday morning the minister's wife had a very strong impression that the woman who had not heard her husband preach and two men from the committee would be in church that day. This, in fact, did happen. One interesting thing about this particular visit is that it was the only one of the visits that members of the committee made with the minister before which they did not telephone him to inform him that they would be in his church on a particular Sunday. This experience involved me, my wife, and the pastoral nominating committee of the church I am now serving.

There is a grandfather clock in my living room that has been in my family for five generations. At the time when the wife of the original owner, my great-great grandfather, died in a hospital near their home, it was reported that the clock struck several times, even though the time was not close to the hour, the only time that the clock normally strikes. To the best of my knowledge, the clock has never acted in this strange way since that day.

The essential question is whether these incidents truly are examples of ESP.

I have to admit that other explanations are possible. In the first two incidents, the fact that family members were ill was known to the percipients, and it would be natural that they might think of death. The fact that it did work out as they thought could be coincidence. On the other hand, the percipients would affirm that these feelings or communications were not just passing thoughts or impressions but that they were so strong that a sense of certainty was established. The example involving the pulpit nominating committee must be handled in the same way. It is natural that a minister or his wife would expect a visit from one person on a committee considering him for their church if that person was the only one who had not heard him preach. My wife and I had discussed this possibility. The fact that it worked out as it did could be simply coincidence. But my wife would affirm that although she thought of this possibility at other times, she had a certain feeling of surety about it only on that one occasion.

One other type of ESP experience should be added to those above. This comes from Dr. Louisa Rhine's collection.

About a year ago my mother drove her Oldsmobile to church and parked in the Churchyard. After Mass, she discovered the car missing, so there was nothing else to do but ride home with friends and phone the police. After searching, the police told us to resign ourselves to the fact that the car must have been taken over the state line. At that time there was quite a racket going on with stolen cars. They were taken to a different state and "stripped" and painted.

My mother's car was a beautiful job with all the accessories imaginable; also it had an expensive jack and two brand-new tires in the trunk. Because it was such a gem, the police doubted we would ever get it back. Although I have my own "Olds," I was especially sick about the whole thing because I used to drive it myself.

Two nights later I dreamed about the car and just what street in Cleveland it would be located on. At that time I was living in a suburb about fifteen miles outside of Cleveland. After telling my husband and phoning my parents about the dream, I drove to this certain street in the center of Cleveland and found the car. As you know, Cleveland is a very large city with hundreds of streets; yet I knew exactly which street to drive to.

The car had been driven over a hundred miles, and had been involved in an accident, but was still in top form. The neighbors in the vicinity told me that the car had been parked there only five minutes before I arrived. I called the police to make out a report, so this incident is in the police files of Cleveland.[3]

Another personal experience is similar to this although it is of somewhat questionable value from the scientific point of view. A friend told my wife of her practice of attempting to visualize the street on which she wanted to park when she was driving into the neighboring city. When she did this, she could "see" if parking spaces were available and where they were located. At the time my wife was going to a nearby city each Monday evening for rehearsal with a choral group, and she always experienced difficulty finding a place to park. She began to practice what her friend did, and she discovered that over a period of twelve weeks each Monday evening she could accurately visualize where a parking space would be available, even though she was still two or three blocks away. Although this has little scientific value, since one can hardly set up a controlled situation to test if ESP actually operated in this situation, it may have some practical value for persons who spend a lot of time searching for parking spaces.

These natural (or unnatural) events may serve as illustrations of the different categories of ESP. Although the term ESP is sometimes used to refer to all paranormal experiences, in a technical sense it is only one of two divisions in the field of parapsychology. The two main divisions in this new field of investigation are extrasensory perception (ESP) and psychokinesis (PK). Extrasensory perception is a phenomenon in which information is by some means perceived about a thought or an event that has happened or will happen which at the moment of perception is totally beyond the reach of the normal channels of sensory experience. Psychokinesis is the ability of the mind alone, with no known physical contact, to exercise some control over a physical object; this is what is commonly called "mind over matter." In addition, ESP may be divided into three categories: telepathy, clairvoyance, and precognition. Telepathy is an interaction between the mind (or body) of one person and the mind (or body) of another person by which information is received through no known sensory apparatus. Clairvoyance is an interaction between one person's mind (or body) and a material event by which information concerning the event is perceived by means other than the known sensory apparatus. Precognition is knowing that an event will occur before it does and therefore before it can be perceived through the known sensory channels.

Of the previously recounted events, the one involving the grandfather clock is the only example that suggests the PK phenomenon. Here the mind of the dying person or the event of death appears to have had some influence on the striking mechanism of the clock. This assumption is supported by the fact that similar unusual events have coincided with other deaths.[4] The other incidents reported from personal experience are examples of the three categories of ESP. Examples of telepathy are the perception of the uncle's death and the knowledge of the visit of the woman and two men from the pastoral nominating committee. The account from Dr. Louisa Rhine's book and the "envisioning" of available parking spaces are examples of clairvoyance. Precognition is illustrated by my wife's realization that her mother would not leave the hospital alive.

These and similar events raise a difficult question. How does ESP occur? No answer can be given at this time for this question. G. D. Wassermann has constructed a theory that utilizes field theory from the theoretical constructs of modern physics.[5] But there is no substantial evidence now available to support this theory. Indeed, there is no definite information to indicate how ESP occurs. No known physical forces convey the information, and no known sensory apparatus perceives it. Yet many people believe that if ESP does occur, some undiscovered physical force and apparatus are responsible for this phenomenon. But before these matters can be explored, a prior question must be asked: Does ESP actually occur?

ESP IN THE LAB

Although Dr. Joseph B. Rhine was not the first person to do experimental work in the field of parapsychology, he is recognized today as a pioneer in this research. Trained in the field of biology, Dr. Rhine and his wife, Louisa, who, like her husband, has a doctorate in biology, became interested in paranormal phenomena in the decade of the 1920's. He joined the psychology department at Duke University and there carried on laboratory experiments to test the possibility of ESP. In 1934 he published a book, *Extra-sensory Perception*,[6] reporting on his experimental work. A storm of controversy developed over this report and the significance of Dr. Rhine's experiments; this controversy is still alive more than thirty-five years later.

The experiments that Dr. Rhine and his colleagues designed utilized a deck of twenty-five cards created by himself and Dr. Karl E. Zener. These cards, known as the Zener cards, have five sets of five cards, each of which has one of five symbols: a circle, a rectangle, a plus sign, a star, and parallel wavy lines. The operational theory Dr. Rhine used was that a person identifying the cards without seeing them would normally get five right in a run through the whole deck of twenty-five cards. With five symbols a person would have one chance in five of correctly identifying the symbol on any single card; in a run of twenty-five cards he could expect to get five right (one fifth of twenty-five). This is the level of chance. If a person could consistently score above the chance level, this would indicate that some extrasensory phenomenon was operating in this situation.

Dr. Rhine, in the beginning, used three experimental techniques. In the Basic Technique (BT) the pack was shuffled, cut, and placed face downward on the table. The subject attempted to guess the first card, which was then removed and placed face downward on a separate pile. A record of the calls was made and then checked against the cards after all twenty-five calls had been made. The second technique was known as Down Through (DT). In this experiment the pack was shuffled, cut, and placed face downward on the table, and the subject guessed the cards one by one from the top without disturbing the pack. These two techniques are tests for pure clairvoyance (PC).[7] Clairvoyance, as noted above, is the interaction between a person's mind and a material event (in this case, a deck of cards) in which information concerning the event is perceived by means other than the known sensory apparatus. In another technique a test was made for pure telepathy (PT), an interaction between the minds of two persons by which information is conveyed through no known sensory apparatus. No cards or records of targets were used, but an agent would at a given moment choose at random an image of one of the five Zener symbols and the subject would record his guess of what the symbol was.[8]

Using these experimental techniques, Dr. Rhine and his associates got spectacular results with certain subjects. This chapter is too brief to include these results in detail, but some record of them is appropriate. A. J. Linzmayer was an undergraduate student in Duke University when he began work with Dr. Rhine. The early experiments with Mr. Linzmayer yielded the best results. In these experiments, which took place in 1931, he achieved 238 hits in 600 trials for a 9.9 average for each 25 trials. This is significantly above the chance level of 5 hits per 25 trials. His best run was 21 out of 25 with fifteen consecutive hits. This run and some others were made in an automobile with the motor running, which would effectively submerge any involuntary auditory clues. Other tests were made with the cards screened from the subject's view, thereby eliminating any possible visual clues. There was no difference in scores on these runs from the scores on others in which the backs of the cards were visible or the motor noise was not blocking any possible involuntary whispering.[9] Tests with Mr. Linzmayer were held on three other occasions after the initial runs in the spring of 1931. He never again approached the high scores he first achieved. He made 6.5 hits per 25 in October, 1931, 6.7 hits per 25 in March, 1932, and 5.9 per 25 in March, 1933. Yet considering all the experimental results with Linzmayer, the odds in favor of the ESP factor, and against chance, are well beyond the trillions, well into the zone of entire statistical validity.[10]

Dr. Rhine reports on his work with eight major subjects in his first book. The subject who did the greatest amount of work in the greatest variety of conditions was Hubert E. Pearce, Jr., a young ministerial student in the Duke School of Religion. The first tests with Mr. Pearce brought scores at only chance level, but after the first one hundred trials his scoring began to rise. In late spring of 1932, Pearce ran 2,250 calls under pure clairvoyance conditions, with the remarkable average per 25 of 9.7, almost double the chance average. His totals up to April 1, 1933, were 11,250 trials, with an average of 8.9 hits per 25.[11] The odds against chance for this are astronomical.

One segment of the experimental work with Pearce must be singled out for special comment. This work has been labeled the Pearce-Pratt experiment after Pearce, the subject, and J. G. Pratt, the agent. In these tests there was distance of over one hundred yards between the agent and the subject. Mr. Pratt, the agent, was in the Physics Building at Duke University, and Mr. Pearce, the subject, was in the Duke Library. The basic technique was used in this long-distance experiment. At a predetermined time Mr. Pratt picked up a card from a shuffled pack of Zener cards, and he continued through the pack at the rate of one card per minute. He did not look at the cards but laid them face down in the center of the table. After each run of 25, Mr. Pratt recorded the order of the cards from the stack in the center of the table. Meanwhile, Mr. Pearce tried to perceive the card Mr. Pratt had exposed. His successes in successive rounds of 25 calls were: 3, 8, 5, 9, 10, 12, 11, 12, 11, 13, 13, 12. From the total of 300 calls Mr. Pearce averaged 9.9 per 25, an average that excludes the chance hypothesis.[12]

This experiment has been singled out as one of the classic experiments that prove that ESP truly is a human phenomenon that can be studied scientifically. The odds against these results arising by chance are greater than 10^{22} to 1. The work with Pearce continued for a short time after Dr. Rhine had published his book. Then one day Pearce received a letter that distressed him greatly, and after this incident he lost his ESP ability.

Dr. Rhine conducted another significant experiment to test ESP over a long distance, this time 250 miles from

Durham to Lake Junaluska, North Carolina. The two participants were Miss Turner and Miss Ownbey, and the experiment took place in July, 1933. At a prearranged time Miss Ownbey started down through a shuffled deck of Zener cards, taking one from the pile every five minutes. The agent's record and subject's record were to be mailed to Dr. Rhine, but on the first three attempts Miss Turner misunderstood and mailed her record to Miss Ownbey. Since the results on these three were outstanding, critics have suggested that Miss Ownbey altered the subject's record before she turned it over to Dr. Rhine. In defense of Miss Ownbey, Dr. Rhine verifies the fact that the entire record was in Miss Turner's handwriting and there was no evidence to suggest fraud. The results on these tests were 19, 16, 16, 7, 7, 8, 6, 2, or an average of 10.1 per 25, which is 10.8 times the probability error and well above chance expectancy.[13]

Some general comments are appropriate concerning some further discoveries that Dr. Rhine made about ESP. One discovery has been the tendency among a number of good telepathic subjects to lose their ability after a period of very good results.[14] This occurred with Linzmayer, Pearce, and other subjects who had given evidence of excellent ESP ability. Pearce's decline, which was so dramatic, coincided with disturbing news received in a letter. ESP ability, most experimenters agree, seems to be related to psychological factors, and anything that might have a psychological effect—shock, boredom, fatigue— could have an influence on ESP ability. Yet this decline phenomenon remains somewhat mysterious. It is difficult to explain why a person who has exhibited unusual ability with ESP should lose that ability after a time and be unable to regain it.

Another interesting phenomenon that Dr. Rhine discovered is what he calls negative ESP. Tests were run in which subjects were instructed to try not to hit the right card. With these instructions some high-scoring subjects slipped to below chance level. Linzmayer in the low-scoring experiment had an average of 4.4 hits per 25,[15] and Pearce had only 20 hits in 275 trials, 35 below chance level.[16] Pearce had the ability to make a high-scoring run of 25 trials and then a low-scoring run of the same number of trials. On one occasion he followed a 9 per 25 high-scoring test with a 1 per 25 low-scoring test. He had one perfect run, calling 0 for 25 in a low-scoring test as well as 25 for 25 in a high-scoring test.[17] Both of these runs are highly significant.

Dr. Rhine ran some tests with his subjects under the influence of certain drugs to determine if they would affect a person's ESP ability. Sodium amytal, a drug that induces sleepiness, reduced dramatically the rate of scoring that subjects had achieved. A large dose of the drug reduced Linzmayer from his high level to the level of chance. In these drug experiments, when caffeine was given to counter the effect of the sodium amytal, the scoring was raised toward the level the subjects had maintained but not above it. It was found, too, that illness reduced the level of scoring.[18] It seems that the factors which create weariness—sodium amytal, fatigue, and illness—reduce the scores on ESP tests, whereas caffeine, which increases alertness, tends to bring scores back toward but not above the previous scoring level. It may be safely concluded that sleepiness reduces ESP ability.

One further observation that Dr. Rhine made from his early experiments that has remained valid for other experimenters is that a subject's ability to concentrate has a positive effect upon his score. Dr. Rhine expressed his

conviction that concentration is the most important
mental condition associated with success in ESP.[19]

The ability to relax and center attention on the experiment increases a person's ESP ability. Distractions, on the
other hand, diminish ESP scores. This factor becomes
very important in evaluating experiments. The presence
of unfamiliar persons or uncomfortable conditions tends
to lower the scoring level of subjects.

Another series of experiments conducted by Dr. Rhine,
which are not reported in his first book, deserve mention:
the Pratt-Woodruff experiments, which were conducted
in 1939. A number of subjects were used in these experiments. The subject sat on one side of a table, which was
divided by a large screen, and J. G. Pratt sat behind him
acting as an observer. At the beginning of each run Mr.
Pratt hung on the screen five ESP cards, each with a
different symbol. These were visible to himself and the
subject, but J. L. Woodruff, who was on the other side
of the screen, could not see them. Mr. Woodruff had in
his possession a shuffled deck of ESP cards. There was a
small opening between the screen and the table, and it
was the subject's task to point through the opening with
a pointer directly beneath the card on the screen having
the symbol he believed was on the top card of the deck.
The deck itself was face down and was screened from
the subject's view. Mr. Woodruff would then take the top
card from the deck and place it where the subject had
pointed. After a run of 25 guesses had been checked, Mr.
Pratt would change the order of the key cards hanging
on the screen, and Mr. Woodruff would shuffle and cut the
deck. In 2,400 runs using this procedure, there were 489
more hits on the target than mean chance expectation. The
chance probability for these results is one in 500,000.[20]

The experiments that Dr. Rhine conducted created a

storm of controversy. Critics who could not believe in the possibility of ESP attacked his methods. They suggested that the backs of the cards used in experiments had printing irregularities and therefore gave sensory clues to subjects. This explanation seemed plausible when it was shown that some cards had such irregularities. Other critics complained of inadequate supervision of experiments when only one person observed the experiment and checked the results. Some suggested that fraud was a possibility and that inadequate precautions were taken to prevent fraud. As these criticisms were made, Dr. Rhine and his staff improved their experimental procedure by doing everything possible to see that sensory clues were excluded and adequate supervision was given. When these steps were taken, scores on ESP experiments declined, and Dr. Rhine has had no subjects since 1939 score as spectacularly as did some between 1930 and 1939. This, say the critics, proves that what has been called ESP really results from subtle sensory clues unconsciously perceived or from fraud. Dr. Rhine has a different explanation. Writing in 1964 about his book *Extra-sensory Perception*, he recalls the "spirit" that infected his staff in the early days of their work together. There was enthusiasm and a spirit of fun that motivated the staff and their subjects. But this motivation was lost in the years of conflict and controversy.

"Attention concentrated on disputes over experimental precautions, interpretation of results, and the like; and, in the years of tension and contention, the wonderful good fun of the early Duke days was lost and forgotten. It never came back to the Duke Laboratory, where the ramparts had to be 'manned for defense' for so many later years. Only in recent times have the old workers begun to call attention to the importance of the psychological atmosphere of testing, the prime importance of strong motivation in the subject, and to recall what has been lost over the years of shifting emphasis."[21]

At about the same time that the results in Dr. Rhine's experimental work began to decline, a new experimenter who achieved significant results appeared in England. His name is S. G. Soal, and the record of his work is contained in two books: *Modern Experiments in Telepathy* and *The Mind Readers*. The first of these books reports the experiments made with two subjects, Basil Shackleton and Mrs. G. Stewart.

S. G. Soal began his ESP experiments with a skeptical attitude, and his experiments with Basil Shackleton at first were not productive. Then, at the suggestion of another experimenter, he began to check what he called +1 and +2 responses. He found that Shackleton seemed to be moving ahead of him as he took cards from the deck and that his response a significant number of times corresponded with the card under the top one (+1) or the card that was second below the top one (+2). With this significant observation Soal began experimenting in earnest.

He followed the same basic procedure as did Dr. Rhine, but he exercised more care in his experimental procedure, thereby reducing the possibility of fraud. He used five cards, each with a picture of one of five animals: elephant, giraffe, lion, pelican, and zebra. The experiments took place in Shackleton's basement apartment in London. The subject, Shackleton, was seated at a table in one room with a recording sheet and pencil before him. An observer sat with him. In the adjoining room out of the line of sight sat an agent at a table on which there was a large screen with an opening (window) in it. On one side of the table sat the experimenter, who exposed through the window of the screen a digit (1 to 5) taken in order from a previously randomized list. The experimenter also signaled the subject that he should record another try. When the digit appeared in the window of the screen, the agent seated on the other side of the screen at the table with five cards before him lifted the card corresponding to the digit shown. After two runs of 25 trials each, the results were compared.

The level of achievement in these experiments were not so spectacular as that for some of Dr. Rhine's subjects, but because of the large number of experiments, the results were quite significant. There were more that 11,000 guesses recorded, and average for this was better than 6.1 hits per 25 calls. The odds against chance for these results are at least ten million to one.[22]

After a time Basil Shackleton's ability as an ESP subject declined. Then Soal began work with another promising subject, Mrs. G. Stewart. The experimental procedure was similar, as were the results. In all, Mr. Soal ran 3,200 trials, and Mrs. Stewart had 759 direct hits in these trials. This is 119 above chance expectation and an average of 5.9 hits per 25 calls. The odds that these results are due to chance alone are over two million to one.[23]

One series of experiments that Mr. Soal designed with Mrs. Stewart as the subject is of special interest. In these experiments, unknown to Mrs. Stewart, Mr. Soal used two agents. He began the series with one agent; then after several runs he had a second agent enter the situation using different cards. When the two agents were in opposition, there was no indication at all that Mrs. Stewart made any contact whatever with the opposition agent. The main effect of the opposition experiments suggests that Mrs. Stewart subconsciously directed her attention exclusively to one of the two agents and ignored the other. There is something here that is akin to the notion of "rapport." [24] This does show that in an experimental situation, and presumably therefore in a natural situation, two minds may make a contact that is not influenced by the thoughts in other persons' minds.

It is significant to note, too, that Mr. Soal carried out one set of experiments with Mrs. Stewart that covered a distance of two hundred miles from Antwerp to London. Mrs. Stewart was in Antwerp on a holiday, and from there she was able to achieve significant results with an agent in London.[25]

By far the most significant results in any ESP experiments are to be found in *The Mind Readers*, S. G. Soal's account of his experiments with two Welsh boys, Ieuan and Glyn Jones. The boys, who are cousins, were in their mid-teens in 1955 to 1957, when the experiments were conducted. Mr. Soal had known these boys and their families for many years, having spent vacations in their home. Quite unexpectedly, in 1955 he discovered that these boys had the ability to guess the five animal symbols on a deck of twenty-five cards.

The experiments Mr. Soal conducted with these boys produced phenomenal results. There was a total of 15,358 trials in these experiments. The number of correct guesses is 5,461 compared with a mean chance expectancy of 3,069.6. The deviation is 2,391.4 above chance. Such a score practically precludes the possibility of chance.[26] To illustrate how phenomenal these results are, in 700 runs of 25 calls the boys twice achieved perfect scores, 25 hits for 25 tries. They scored between 20 and 25 hits twenty-four times, and they hit 12 to 19 one hundred and fifty-three times. In a quarter of their calls they were scoring more than double the level of chance.[27]

It would seem that such results would speak for themselves, but there are two factors in these experiments that must be considered in evaluating the results: they could not score above chance when a door was closed between them, and they were caught cheating.

Ieuan and Glyn, it was discovered early in the experiments, could not achieve high scores when they were in adjoining rooms with the door closed. When the boys were thoroughly screened from each other and the door was open, they would score high. As soon as the door was closed, their scores would drop to the level of chance. When the door was opened again, the scores would go up. This situation suggests that some auditory or visual clues accounted for the high scores. But Soal and those who worked with him were very careful to observe every sound and move, and they verify that no such clues could have been given. Their explanation of this phenomenon is that somehow a closed door was a psychological inhibition that lowered the boys' ability to score well.[28] Some of the experiments were conducted in a situation in which the boys were screened completely from each other's view, and some were conducted in an open field when the boys were screened from each other and separated by a distance up to one hundred feet. The high scores achieved on these occasions would seemingly rule out the fact that sensory clues were responsible for the boys' success.

But were the results phenomenal because of fraud? This is a question that must be given serious consideration, because Ieuan and Glyn were caught cheating.

In November and December of 1955, the boys employed a crude form of cheating by using a simple auditory code that was easily detected. As the cards were exposed, a creak of the chair indicated a lion, a stamp on the floor meant a zebra, two stamps was a giraffe, a loud cough was a pelican, and silence indicated an elephant.[29] The boys were confronted with their deceit and contritely admitted their guilt. The experimenters were doubly watchful after that and never again detected any form of cheating. On one occasion cards with different symbols— soldier, policeman, boy, racing car, and view of St. Paul's Cathedral in London—were unexpectedly introduced for one series of tests. The boys could not have arranged a code for these symbols, yet their results for eight runs averaged 11 per 25 tries. The odds against chance for these experiments are at least 10^{15} to one.[30] Perhaps of greater significance is the fact that one series of tests was held in the presence of three experienced psychic re- searchers, of whom one, Jack Salvin, was an expert in detecting fraudulent telepathy. These researchers were unable to detect any cheating.[31] The scores for these tests were equal to those in other successful experiments.

Mr. Soal and his staff had encountered great difficulty in personal relationships with Ieuan and Glyn and the members of their families. The relationship seemed too difficult to continue, and the experiments drew to a close after two years. Yet these experiments have produced results that are more significant than any other ones.

CRITICISM AND CONTROVERSY

The results of ESP experiments have not been accepted with enthusiasm in scientific circles. Numerous suggestions have been made by critics to explain away the results. Some objections have been mentioned. The "unconscious whispering" theory was an early suggestion. Those who advanced this theory said that the agent unconsciously whispered what symbol was on the card and the subject subconsciously picked up this sensory clue and was able to give the correct answer more often than chance expectation. The distance experiments have put this theory to rest. Critics have suggested, too, that the mathematical methods of evaluation were inaccurate, but this was proved false. Others said shuffling did not bring a random distribution, and subjects could follow the arrangement of the cards from one run to another. This criticism has been checked and found invalid. Still other critics would explain significant results as errors in recording and checking, but again competent and impartial persons have proved that such errors are minimal and insignificant.

There remains one theory to explain away the significant results in ESP experiments—fraud. This is the line of attack followed by C. E. M. Hansel in his book *ESP: A Scientific Evaluation*.[32] Dr. Hansel investigates the significant ESP experiments conducted by Dr. Rhine and Mr. Soal, and shows how the results could have been attained fraudulently. In the Pratt-Pearce experiments Dr. Hansel suggests that Pearce, who was in the library, could have come to the classroom building where Pratt had the cards. While Pratt recorded the cards, Pearce, by standing in a chair and looking through a transom, could have recorded his calls.[33] He shows how fraud could have accounted for the excellent results in the other Duke experiments. Mr. Soal receives the same skeptical treatment. Dr. Hansel suggests that the results of the Soal experiments with Mr. Shackleton could have been achieved by fraud if Mr. Shackleton and one agent had agreed to work together.[34] The same explanation holds for Mr. Soal's experiments with Mrs. Stewart.[35] Of course, the argument of fraud in the case of Soal's excellent results with Ieuan and Glyn Jones is enhanced by the fact that they were detected cheating and that they could not score well when a closed door came between them. Hansel further suggests that the boys used a "silent" dog whistle to communicate on certain of the outdoor distance tests.[36] Dr. Hansel stops short of denying the existence of ESP. What he says is that even the best experiments are not sufficient to prove scientifically that ESP is a fact.[37]

Dr. Hansel's criticism must be taken seriously. However, it is also fair to indicate that while he does show how fraud could have operated in these experiments, sometimes his explanations, such as Pearce's standing on a chair to view cards through a transom, sound a bit ridiculous. Furthermore, he "stacks the deck" in favor of his thesis by avoiding mention of the very careful precautions taken to eliminate fraud in many of these experiments.

After weighing the evidence and considering the adverse criticisms, it is my opinion that ESP is a phenomenon that has been observed in natural situations and adequately demonstrated in laboratory experiments.

PERSONAL EXPERIMENTS

In the autumn months of 1968, seven girls from a youth organization I was advising volunteered to participate in some ESP experiments. At that time I had done very little reading in this field, and I knew nothing about the accepted procedures for testing. As a result, supervision in these experiments was not adequate, and the results of the experiments could not be accepted in scientific circles.

The experiments were conducted at an open doorway. The subject and the agent were seated facing the same direction (toward the open doorway) on either side of the wall that led to the door. They were only a few feet apart, but they were completely screened from each other's view. A third person, a recorder, sat in the doorway facing the agent and the subject. Her task was to record the tries. The agent had five cards on which were the digits 1 to 5. She would take one card, turn it over, and then show it to the recorder. The recorder indicated to the subject that she should make her guess. After the call had been made, the recorder would write down the number shown and the call. When fifty calls were completed, the hits were recorded. On about a quarter of the tries the procedure was varied by moving the agent twenty feet from the doorway and using two recorders, one to record the card the agent chose and the other to record the call the subject made.

Numerous objections could be made to this procedure. In most of the experiments one person was recording both the numbers chosen and the calls made. In addition, numbers were not randomized in a way that would assure that perceivable patterns would not appear, and there was not adequate supervision to assure that cheating did not occur. As the experimenter, I am sure that there was no fraud, but I cannot prove this.

Inadequate as the design of the experiments was, the results were phenomenal. Between 350 and 400 tries were made with each girl as subject. Five girls scored only at the chance level, but two scored well above the level of chance (how well above I did not realize until a year later). One made 164 hits in 350 tries, and another made 149 hits in 400 tries. I used the formulae in Mr. Soal's book [38] to evaluate these results. These formulae are Standard Deviation equals 0.4 times the square root of the number of guesses, and Critical Ratio equals the numerical deviation divided by the standard deviation. The critical ratio then is checked on a table to get the odds of this happening by chance. In one case, the standard deviation for 164 hits in 350 tries is 7.48 and the numerical deviation (hits above chance level) is 94. The critical ratio for her work is 12.6, which is so high it is not on Mr. Soal's table of odds against chance. The odds would be astronomical that this score could be attained by chance. In the other case, the standard deviation for 194 hits in 400 tries is 8. The numerical deviation (hits above chance level) is 69. The critical ratio then is 8.6. On Mr. Soal's table the highest critical ratio given is 8.0 and the odds for this critical ratio are shown as 8.3×10^{14} to one. It is practically impossible to ascribe these results to chance, and as an experimenter I am reasonably satisfied that there was no fraud. I believe that these results indicate the existence of ESP.

I made additional attempts at some ESP experiments after I had become better acquainted with the published material in parapsychology. One set of experiments seemed to be promising, but after the first runs scoring fell to chance level. These tests involve my oldest child, David, who was within weeks of his tenth birthday when the tests occurred.

The setting for the experiments was the family room–

dining room area of our home. David, the subject, sat at the table in our family room. His mother, the agent, sat at the table in our dining room. The door was open between the two rooms, but they were totally screened from each other's view by the partition between the rooms. I stood in the doorway between the rooms to inform my wife when David was ready for the next try.

On the table before my wife were five cards numbered 1 through 5. On the faces of the five cards were pictures of animals—eagle, giraffe, zebra, pig, and lion. My wife had a list of random numbers, 1 through 5, prepared by using the next to the last figure in a column of numbers from the telephone book. When David was ready for a try, she would turn over the card corresponding to the next figure on the sheet of random numbers, and David would record his guess. Then I would signal that he was ready for the next trial.

The first time the experiment was run, David made scores of 7, 5, 8, and 9 per 25. The standard deviation for these runs is four, and the critical ratio is 2.25, with odds against chance of about 30 to 1. Two weeks later on two successive evenings a hundred trials were run. The results for the first evening were 7, 4, 5, and 3 per 25, and those for the second evening were 7, 5, 7, and 2. These scores taken together are exactly at the level of chance. The standard deviation for the total 300 trials is nearly 7, and the actual deviation is 9. The critical ratio for all 300 trials is not significant.

An interesting observation that bears on these experiments is that the first hundred trials were made in the afternoon immediately after lunch. The trials on the second two occasions were made at bedtime when the other children were in bed and the house was quiet. On those two occasions, low scores (3 and 2) occurred on the final run of 25. It may be that at that point fatigue or boredom was inhibiting David's ESP ability.

Very little has been mentioned yet about PK, psychokinesis. Dr. Rhine has designed experiments using dice to test for the possibility of PK. In rolling a die, there is one chance in six that a particular face will appear. In a run of 24 throws with one die, the chance level expectation is that each face will turn up four times. If, in a long series of runs, a person would concentrate on one face (number) and it would appear more often than chance expectation, this would indicate the existence of a PK factor. Beginning in 1934, Dr. Rhine and his staff experimented with dice in PK experiments. Mrs. Rhine totals the results of the PK experiments that her husband and his staff conducted between 1934 and 1941. In those experiments there were 651,216 die throws or 27,134 runs. In this high number of runs the hits show a deviation above chance, which produced odds of 10^{115} to 1 against attributing these results to chance.[39] The results in the PK experiments have been questioned by critics who say Dr. Rhine did not consider any natural inclination that the dice might have to turn up a certain number more often than chance expectation.

I attempted to duplicate Dr. Rhine's PK experiments. I selected six dice which I put into a cup in which they were shaken, and then rolled them down a 45 degree incline onto the top of the dining room table, which had a pad and a cloth on it. I first rolled the dice 48 times without trying for any number, and I recorded what faces appeared on all the dice on each of these throws. I discovered that certain numbers appeared more often than others, some appearing above chance expectation and some below. In these 48 rolls the following scores for each face were made: 1's—44 times, 2's—55 times, 3's—43 times, 4's—53 times, 5's—45 times, 6's—48 times. I then rolled the dice 288 times, concentrating on each of the six numbers for 48 tries. The results I got were not significantly different from the trial rolls: 1's—45 times, 2's—52 times, 3's—45 times, 4's—46 times, 5's—48 times, 6's—45 times. There was no real evidence in these experiments to indicate the presence of a PK factor.

As a result of these personal experiments, I believe I have accumulated some evidence that would support the conclusion that ESP is a factor in human experience. On the other hand, I have personally discovered no evidence to support the existence of a PK factor, but I must admit that my experiments were not so well designed, nor were they so extensive, as Dr. Rhine's were.

THEORETICAL CONSIDERATIONS FOR ESP

To this point alternative explanations for what purports to be ESP have been considered. The unconscious whispering theory must be discarded, since ESP ability has been demonstrated between two people separated by distances of up to two hundred miles. The theory that subtle sensory clues are responsible for positive results in ESP experiments likewise is ruled out by the distance experiments and by the numerous tests in which the cards have been screened completely from the subject's view. Fraud is the most difficult counterexplanation to handle. Fraud could be an explanation. However, it seems that positive results have been received by numerous experimenters in carefully controlled situations. After reading accounts of all these experiments and achieving positive results in some experiments conducted personally, it is difficult to doubt the integrity of all these persons. In addition to the laboratory experiments, there are on record thousands of occurrences of ESP in natural situations, and these alone may be sufficient evidence for ESP. One may safely conclude that there is no satisfactory counterexplanation for ESP.

Why, then, does controversy continue? Why do reasonable men refuse to accept the evidence from laboratory and life for ESP? There appear to be four reasons for this. First, it seems that the evidence fails to convince many people because they have an irrational prejudice against the concept of ESP. Various books have carried comments by persons who have said that even if the laboratory experiments for ESP were conclusive, they would not believe that ESP is a factor in human experience. This concept simply does not fit their world view. One survey taken in 1952 showed that only one in six psychologists accepted the occurrence of ESP. Of those who rejected the concept, two thirds admitted they had never read an original report of experiments and one third admitted they had made up their minds without ever considering the evidence at all.[40] It seems that the opposition to the acceptance of the ESP concept stems from the belief fostered by science that everything must have a demonstrably physical cause. A closed scientific system and a closed mind rule out the possibility of ESP. But such systems and attitudes are themselves quite unscientific.

The acceptance of the concept of ESP does necessitate some basic rethinking and restructuring of one's concept of the universe. The rather rigid space-time concept of the universe is shattered by the ESP concept. This concept not only affirms communication from mind to mind or from event to mind through no known sensory apparatus but also reveals that space is no limitation at all to ESP. The ability to perceive through ESP, it seems, does not decline as distance increases. ESP is space free. But even more difficult to accept than its space-free nature is the fact that ESP may be time free. In the space-time world of physics the two, space and time, go together; every physical force consumes time as it travels from place to place in space. It should follow, then, that what is space free would also be time free. Precognition may indicate this about ESP.

The important problem raised by precognition is that if something can be known before it occurs, such perception simply cannot be physical in any current sense of that word. I included the precognitive phenomenon in the personal examples at the beginning of this chapter, but I have not yet given any examples of experiments to support this aspect of ESP. Dr. Rhine ran some precognition tests with Mr. Pearce in which he asked him to make his calls through a deck of Zener cards not as the deck was at that time but as it would be after it was shuffled and cut. Mr. Pearce's rate of success was significantly above chance level—6.3 hits per run in one series of 212 runs and 7.1 hits per run in another series of 223 runs.[41] A problem arose, however, when some of Dr. Rhine's assistants suggested and then demonstrated that when a person shuffled the cards, some ESP factor seemed to influence the shuffling so that the order of the cards in the shuffled deck would match the order in a target deck more frequently than chance would allow. This meant that Mr. Pearce's list of calls could influence positively the shuffling that was done subsequently to form the target deck. When this factor was recognized, Dr. Rhine designed a more complex experiment in which mechanical shuffling was used, and he still got positive results for precognition.[42] Another more sophisticated precognition experiment in which subjects guess a 100 digit number that will be produced at random by a computer is reported later in this chapter.

There is, then, some natural and experimental evidence to support precognition, indicating that ESP is time free as well as space free. What does this indicate about our world? There are three possible explanations. It could mean that time is an illusion in human experience. It could mean that events in the world are to some degree guided or determined by mind(s) that is on a different plane from human minds. Or it could mean that the human mind can perceive certain factors by ESP, evaluate them subconsciously, and produce consciously an accurate prediction of what will happen. Dr. Rhine has said that he believes that the precognition hypothesis is likely to be one of the great battlegrounds of science, for nothing is more truly revolutionary or radically contradictory to contemporary thought than this hypothesis.[43] A large obstacle that must be overcome before the concept of ESP will be widely accepted is the resistance of people to any concept that necessitates a rearrangement of their concept of the universe. This is not surprising because it is this factor which has prevented the immediate acceptance of numerous theories about life that have in time been proved true.

A second problem in the acceptance of ESP is that the ESP experiments and the natural occurrences of ESP are not repeatable in the strict scientific sense of that term. A person may perceive by non-sensory means that a relative has died, but on other occasions when other relatives die, for some reason he has no extrasensory perception of that event. Or in the laboratory a person may score well one day, and on another day when conditions appear to be identical, he will score poorly. When a chemist combines certain elements under certain conditions and a reaction takes place, he knows that every time these elements and these conditions are combined he will have a similar reaction. The parapsychologist rarely has that experience. Experimental parapsychology resembles in one way experimental astronomy. In neither science do experiments produce phenomena; tests are simply attempts to catch some part of the occurrence in the field.

A third factor that creates problems for the ESP experimenter and has limited the acceptance of the ESP concept is the fact that the ESP experiments in the first three decades of laboratory work suggested that ESP ability is limited to a few people. Millions of laboratory tests have been conducted with cards and other devices, and most people have been unable to score significantly above the chance level. Nevertheless, it has been clearly demonstrated that a small number of people can score far in excess of probability over sustained periods of time, and this supports the existence of ESP.

Now there is new experimental evidence that indicates that many people may have some measure of ESP ability. Experiments that have revealed this have been conducted by John Mihalasky and E. Douglas Dean at the Newark College of Engineering in Newark, New Jersey. They have used the plethysmograph, which records changes in the circulation of blood in the extremities of the body, in their experiments. Diminution of the volume of blood is interpreted as vasoconstriction, and increase in blood volume as vasodilation. It had been demonstrated that when a person does a short period of mental arithmetic, a vasoconstriction occurs. In 1958, S. Figar, who was running experiments measuring the vasoconstriction and attempting to relate it with mental activity, noticed a curious phenomenon. With several subjects, as soon as Figar thought of picking up the card on which were written instructions about the mental arithmetic but before actually doing so, his thought was followed by a rapid vasoconstriction in the subject's hand. It seemed as if there was some kind of communication between Figar's thoughts and his subject's vasoconstrictions.

Mr. Dean, before he came to the Newark College of Engineering, devised an experiment to test for ESP through the use of the plethysmograph, and he has continued this line of experimentation since assuming his position with the PSI Communication Project at Newark.[44] It was decided that since mental arithmetic may not be reliable in these experiments, names would be used. The person who was the stimulator at the experiment wrote the names of five people of recent emotional relationship with him on cards and the respondent did the same. Added to these ten cards were ten others—five with names taken at random from a telephone book and five that were blank. The respondent then was placed in a laboratory room, where he reclined and had the plethysmograph attached to his finger. The stimulator took the twenty cards to another room in another building an eighth of a mile away. There was no physical connection between the two people. The stimulator then randomized the cards and selected the time intervals between stimulus periods. At the appointed time the stimulator picked up a card and concentrated on the name written on it.

The experiments that have been conducted show that in the case of the blank cards and the cards with names taken from the telephone book there is no measurable change in the pattern recorded on the plethysmograph. But if the name was known to the respondent or to the stimulator, the wave pattern on the recording instrument indicated vasoconstriction, which suggested mental activity stimulated by the thought processes of a person one eighth of a mile away. Mr. Dean has devised an alternate method for this experiment in which the respondent is asleep. The stimulator in this test uses pictures that suggest vertical or horizontal motion or blank sheets suggesting no motion at all. Using an electroencephalograph to record the rapid eye movements (REMs) during dream periods, Mr. Dean has discovered that the direction of the respondent's REMs—vertical or horizontal—coincides with the picture on which the stimulator is concentrating. Again there is positive and measurable evidence for ESP.[45] In the experiment described first, in which both the respondent and the stimulator are awake, Mr. Dean had significant results with at least one out of four persons tested; and in the second experiment, when the respondent is asleep, he had significant results with three out of every four persons tested.[46] This suggests that a majority of people do possess some capacity for ESP. In addition, it is significant that positive results have been achieved by Mr. Dean in experiments in which the stimulator and respondent have been three thousand miles apart.[47]

These experiments pose an interesting problem. In the

experiments in which both the stimulator and the respondent were awake, the names that were meaningful to both of them created a measurable response that was nearly identical in strength. Yet, presumably the names the stimulator chose would be no more meaningful to the respondent than the names from the telephone book, and the names the respondent chose would not be meaningful to the stimulator. It would seem that when the stimulator concentrated on a name meaningful to the respondent, the name itself was communicated to the respondent creating a measurable reaction. But when the stimulator concentrated on a name meaningful to himself, but not to the respondent, his own emotional reaction to the name was communicated to the respondent and created in him sympathetic feelings. This phenomenon needs more exploration, and no doubt in the future experiments will be devised to discover just what kinds of data are communicated through ESP.

It has now been demonstrated that more than a small percentage of people have the capacity for ESP. But the fact that certain people have more ability than others raises the question of a possible link between ESP ability and personality. Do certain personality types possess a greater capacity for ESP than do others? These investigations have been inconclusive, and some researchers think that there is no link between personality and ESP ability. The search for some link between ESP ability and personality has not been completed, but some recent experimental evidence suggests that such a link may exist. Before this evidence is presented, two non-personality factors that do influence ESP ability should be introduced. Both of these have to do with attitude. The one factor involves psychological attitude. The presence of visitors or spectators has inhibited the ability of some subjects. Pressure to continue experiments against a subject's desire has produced negative deviations of significance.[48] ESP tests with children four and ten years old in classrooms have shown that the children's attitudes toward their teacher (the agent) had an influence on ESP ability. The 230 subjects who had favorable feelings toward the teacher had an average score of 5.26 in 1,103 runs, whereas the 149 subjects with a negative attitude toward the teacher had an average score of 4.64 on 708 runs.[49] These results are significant, and they indicate that a psychological factor that distracts or disturbs the subject inhibits his ESP ability.

The other factor that may influence ESP ability is the general attitude one has toward ESP. This factor has been demonstrated by the work of Dr. Gertrude R. Schmeidler. Dr Schmeidler was running some ESP experiments and asked two psychologists among numerous other people to act as subjects. These two psychologists expressed their total disbelief of the concept of ESP, but despite their feelings they did agree to participate in the experiments. Both of them scored fewer successes than would be expected by the chance rate of one out of five. These low scores beside the higher ones of subjects with a favorable attitude toward ESP led to a hypothesis Dr. Schmeidler began to test: that subjects with a favorable attitude toward ESP will make higher scores than those with an unfavorable one. Dr. Schmeidler designated those with a favorable attitude "sheep" and those with an unfavorable attitude "goats." In the first experiments, she made 1,055 runs of 25 with 111 "sheep," and they scored 242 above chance for an average of 5.23 hits per run. In the same tests, she made 853 runs with 40 "goats," and they scored 116 below the level of chance for an average of 4.86 hits per run.[50] Eventually she completed 250,875 ESP card trials with 1,157 subjects, and the results were consistent with the first trials.[51] Additional experiments by other persons have produced similar results. It seems clear that another factor that has an effect on ESP ability is whether or not a person believes in ESP.

To return to the question of a link between personality and ESP ability, one must consider recent precognition experiments conducted by John Mihalasky and E. Douglas Dean at the Newark College of Engineering. These experiments were designed to test the ESP factor in management decisions made by business executives. Since decisions at the higher levels of management are frequently based on unreliable and incomplete data, it was thought that some precognitive factor may assist the successful executive in decision-making.

Business executives were selected for these experiments. They were tested first concerning their acceptance of ESP, that is, whether they were "sheep" or "goats." Then they were asked about their attitude toward time by selecting the one out of five metaphors they liked best —a dashing waterfall, a galloping horseman, an old woman spinning, a vast expanse of sky, a quiet motionless ocean. The waterfall and horseman selection classified the person as having a vectorial attitude toward time or dynamic personality traits; the sky and ocean selections classified the person as having an oceanic attitude toward time or nondynamic personality traits. Then the participants selected a 100 digit number. Since there are ten possible numbers—0 to 9—for each digit, the chance level of scoring hits would be one in ten. The participants were told that their number would be compared with a

100 digit number to be generated by a computer by means of a random number-generating process. A score of over 10 hits would indicate precognitive ability. Twenty experiments were run, involving 954 men. The results were that men in the dynamic category scored an average of 10.17 successes whereas men in the non-dynamic category scored an average of 9.65.[52] These figures do not deviate from chance to a significant degree, but they do indicate a trend. What is significant is that the dynamic category consistently scored higher than the nondynamic one.

In an additional experiment, a positive correlation was demonstrated between high profits in business and above-average scores, which indicates that a precognition test might be a valid tool in the selection of top executives. A tentative conclusion that can be drawn from these experiments is that there may be a link between personality traits and ESP ability. Certainly the final word has not been written on this problem, but what work has been done points in this direction.

A fourth factor that limits the acceptance of the ESP concept is the lack of any theory explaining how the phenomenon occurs. There are some indications that a type of extrasensory perception exists in all of nature. There are many creatures that have a "homing" instinct. There is no conclusive explanation for this; some researchers think that this instinct is sensory, and some believe that it is extrasensory. However, on occasion an animal has found his way to a certain location, and the only possible explanation for this accomplishment is some form of extrasensory perception. J. G. Pratt recounts the experience of the Doolen family, which moved from Aurora, Illinois, forty miles west of Chicago, to Lansing,

Michigan, 175 miles northeast of Chicago. Before they left Aurora, they gave their pet dog "Tony" to friends. Six weeks after they moved, a dog came up to Mr. Doolen on a sidewalk in downtown Lansing. It was Tony.

Another such story involves a boy in West Virginia and his pet pigeon. The boy was taken to a hospital seventy miles from his home. A few days later at dusk during a snowstorm a pigeon appeared at the window of the boy's hospital room. The boy seemed so agitated because a pigeon was there in such bad weather that the nurse acceded to his wish to bring it inside. Then the boy discovered it was his own pet pigeon.[53]

Some recent experiments with plants by Cleve Backster, of the Backster Research Foundation of New York City, suggests that there is a primary "extrasensory" perception that functions among all living things. Mr. Backster, who had received training at the U.S. Army Polygraph School, decided one day after he had watered an office plant that he would try to measure the rate at which water rises in a plant from the roots to the leaf. He chose the psychogalvanic reflex (PGR) index as a possible means of measuring the rate of ascent of the moisture. By attaching a pair of PGR electrodes to a leaf of the plant and bridging these to the polygraph, he hoped to record the increase in the plant leaf's moisture content on the polygraph tape. The tracings on the tape did not exhibit the pattern Mr. Backster anticipated. A few moments later he decided to test what reaction a plant might have if there was a threat to its well being. He immersed the leaf next to the one to which the electrodes were attached in a cup of hot coffee. There was no measurable reaction. Then he decided to get a match to actually burn the plant leaf being tested. At the moment he decided this, but before he made any move to carry out the decision, there was a dramatic change in the tracing pattern in the form of an abrupt and prolonged upward sweep of the recording pen. It seemed the plant reaction recorded on the tracing was caused by the mere thought of harm intended for the leaf.[54]

In subsequent months Mr. Backster devised an experiment in which brine shrimp were killed by dropping them into boiling water in the presence of plants attached to the polygraph, which measured their reaction. When the brine shrimp were dropped, the polygraph needle jumped, recording the reaction of the plant. Presumably this reaction was caused by the death of the shrimp, which would indicate that there is some communication between living organisms that does not utilize known sensory organs. Mr. Backster hypothesizes that this perception facility may be part of a primary sensory system capable of functioning at cell level.[55] In an interview reported in *National Wildlife* magazine, Mr. Backster reports that one time when he was fifteen miles from his office, he merely thought about returning, and at the precise moment that thought crossed his mind there was a coincidental reaction by the plants recorded on the polygraph.[56] It seems that in all levels of life in the natural world there may be some perception that occurs that does not utilize any sensory apparatus now identified.

Another hypothesis that may be substantiated in further ESP research has been advanced by Charles McCreery, of the Institute of Psychophysical Research at Oxford, England. He suggests that the alpha rhythm of the brain measurable on the electroencephalograph is associated with the ESP state. He predicts that the alpha rhythm will be found to be continuous during the production of

ESP.[57] It has been demonstrated that sensory intellectual activity inhibits the alpha rhythm. On the other hand, accelerated alpha frequency is associated with the kind of attention required in the ESP state. Another fact that would suggest a link between the alpha rhythm and the ESP state is that depressant drugs that inhibit ESP slow the alpha rhythm, and stimulant drugs that tend to improve the ESP state accelerate the alpha rhythm. Mr. McCreery presents other evidence that shows a correlation between alpha rhythm and the ESP state. He does not, however, draw the conclusion that the alpha rhythm is the means of extrasensory communication. What he says is that he believes it has something to do with the ESP state, that is, the state in which conscious ESP occurs.[58]

There seems to be a positive correlation between the alpha rhythm and the state in which ESP occurs, but the hypothesis Mr. McCreery presents must be explored further before it can be advanced as a theory.

An interesting experiment involving ESP and the alpha rhythm has been conducted by T. D. Duane and Thomas Behrendt, of Jefferson Medical College. These two doctors concentrated on the occurrence of illness or trauma in one of a pair of identical twins that affects the other, even though the twins are far apart and unaware of what is happening to each other. They placed identical twins in separate rooms and recorded their alpha rhythm on an electroencephalograph. The alpha rhythm can be elicited by having a subject close his eyes, or stare at a uniform, unpatterned background, or sit with eyes open in a dark place. The experimenters chose the simplest method of inducing alpha rhythm and instructed one of the twins to close his eyes at certain time intervals. In two out of fifteen sets of twins tested, the production of the alpha rhythm by one twin's closing his eyes produced the alpha rhythm in the other twin.[59] The doctors further noted that these two pairs of twins were relaxed and unconcerned about the test whereas the other thirteen pairs exhibited some anxiety about it. The experimenters refrain from drawing any conclusions since their results are so meager. But the experiment does demonstrate an extrasensory factor that influences the incidence of alpha brain waves in some pairs of identical twins. The experiment suggests, too, that the alpha rhythm may have something to do with ESP.

The scientific study of parapsychology is presently in the infant stage. The fact of some paranormal force in human experience has been adequately demonstrated; when a measurable physical change can be produced by extrasensory means, one can hardly doubt that ESP occurs. However, none of the basic theory related to paranormal activity has been discovered. The parapsychologist is a scientific pioneer venturing into uncharted areas of human experience. Many significant discoveries remain to be made, but there is little doubt that these discoveries will come in time.

The Practical Value of ESP

A legitimate question to raise is, What practical value does ESP have in human experience? ESP is a curious and interesting phenomenon, but it does not seem to be a reliable form of communication for all occasions.

The interesting possibility that Mr. Mihalasky and Mr. Dean are exploring in their work is that ESP may be used for communication in deep space and deep water work, where conventional methods of communication are deficient. Under certain circumstances in space travel, there are communication blackouts, and in travels into deep space there is a time lag in conventional forms of communication. In deep water, too, heat layers disrupt conventional communication. The experimenters at Newark College of Engineering are testing to see if some form of extrasensory communication may be utilized in these situations. ESP has been used, too, with some success in the detection of criminals, so it could become a tool in crime detection.

But the important application I wish to discuss in this book is the implications of the experiments in ESP and psychic phenomena for the field of religion. When one accepts the fact that there is ESP, he then is forced to admit that there are forces in the universe that are not material, at least in the sense of the current definition given to that word. ESP certainly has some relationship with prayer. It may have implications, too, for survival after death and for spiritual healing. These will be the topics of successive chapters.

3

PRAYER

Some people make an uncritical leap from ESP to prayer —if the ESP phenomena exist, they say, then the claims religious people make about prayer are true. There is, I believe, a relationship between ESP and prayer, but one must make a very careful distinction between the two. Extrasensory perception is communication between or among persons or between an event and a person through means other than the recognized sensory apparatus. But prayer, at least in the traditional sense, is communication between man and God, and most religious teachers see this communication moving in both directions: man to God and God to man. The crucial thing to note is that ESP experiments do not prove the existence of God. They simply indicate that communication may occur by extrasensory means.

But there is one aspect of the ESP phenomena that can point beyond the human plane. That is precognition. The question of precognition arose in the last chapter, and there I indicated that precognition suggests one of three suppositions—time may be an illusion in human experience, or events in the world may be to some degree guided or determined by mind(s) that is on a different plane from human minds, or the mind of the one who has the precognitive experience may gather information from different sources by extrasensory means, evaluate that information subconsciously, and then in the conscious mind perceive what probably will happen.

I want to consider this final possibility first. According to this theoretical construct, a person who perceives, for example, that a plane he is about to board will crash has received by extrasensory perception some piece of information about the airplane—mechanical defect, a bomb planted in a suitcase, or some such problem—and he has subconsciously evaluated this with the result that he "knows" the plane will crash. The difficulty with this hypothesis of what happens in precognition is that sometimes the event conceived beforehand is caused by factors that are not apparent at that moment. Using the same example, people have had the precognitive experience of knowing a plane will crash when that crash was caused by pilot error. Mechanically the plane was in good condition and all other factors were normal. It is difficult to imagine that a person's mind could pick up some bit of information that would lead to the conclusion that a pilot who is competent and always before has made the proper decisions will at a specific moment make a fatal miscalculation.

The example of precognition given in Chapter 2 concerning my wife's perception that her mother would not leave the hospital highlights this problem. Even if my wife had perceived by extrasensory means her mother's condition at that time, her evaluation of that information would not have been that her mother would not leave the hospital. Having grown up in a doctor's home, she knew the course such an illness takes. The fatal embolism probably came as a result of the operation, and this specific condition was not present when my wife had her precognitive experience. It seems, then, that explaining precognition by saying that the mind gathers information by extrasensory means and then in a computerlike fashion evaluates the material and gives a correct answer is not completely plausible, because at times some of the information needed to make that evaluation is not yet available when one has a precognitive experience.

Another possible explanation for precognition is that time is an illusion in human experience. If this were the situation, it would mean that although we perceive things in a temporal sequence, they may not necessarily occur that way when viewed from another plane of existence. The possibility that time is an illusion is a part of some philosophical and theological constructions. When we talk about eternity as a divine attribute or as an experience after death, we usually conceive of this not as the endless extension of time but as the absence of a temporal sequence. But does this construct have a link with anything in human experience? One comparable human experience is reported by a few musicians who claim to perceive a musical event fully in one moment rather than as a sequence of sounds over a period of time. If the sequence of time is an illusion, we can understand how a person's mind can bypass the normal sequential way of perceiving events to perceive something that has occurred on the time-free plane but has not yet occurred on the time-bound plane of human experience. The difficulty with this concept, however, is that there is no conclusive evidence that time is an illusion. Nevertheless, it does remain a possibility. It may be as difficult for us to understand that there is a time-free plane as it would be for a fish to understand that there is a plane of life in which creatures walk on dry land and breathe through lungs.

The third possible explanation for precognition is that a mind(s) to some degree guides or determines what will happen. This information, then, is perceived by extra-sensory means. This theoretical construct requires a "spiritual" or supernatural being(s). It is perhaps the simplest of the three possibilities to conceptualize, but it, too, has its problems. The major problem is the thorny issue that always irritates any person who has seriously considered the Christian doctrine of providence. The problem has been stated in various ways, but basically it is this—if a good God guides or determines events in the world, why is there so much evil? If it is true that events are in some way guided or determined by super-natural forces, one is almost forced to accept the trouble-some theory that there is some mixture of good and evil among these forces or among the beings who wield an influence on events. This posits at least two competitive spiritual forces influencing events, and raises the question of which one predominates. Christian theology has tried to resist such an absolute ethical dualism.

Some precognitive experiences seem to indicate that there is not a strict determinism that operates in human affairs. In one situation a woman perceived that she would have an automobile accident on a certain occasion. Forewarned and fearful, she drove very slowly. At a particular point in that drive her brakes failed, but be-cause she was going slowly she was able to bring the car safely to a stop by drifting to the side of the road and up a small incline. Had she driven at a normal speed, this mechanical failure probably would have resulted in an accident. Another incident involves a father and his daughter. She was visiting friends at a lakeside cottage. Her father, at home, perceived that she would drown that day. He called the cottage to tell her of this precognitive perception, and asked her not to swim that day. She did not. Had she gone swimming, would she have drowned? One cannot say. But these incidents seem to indicate that a precognitive perception does not necessarily mean an event will happen. In other words, events are not predetermined and unchangeable. There is, at least, some element of freedom that operates in human experience.

Precognition is a troubling phenomenon. Each of the three possible theoretical explanations for it presents difficulties. What this discussion does indicate is that precognition and, to a degree, the other ESP phenomena, suggest a class of realities that stand outside the presently defined characteristics of the physical order. This dimension of reality may be called "metaphysical," which literally means "beyond the physical dimension." Some people will consider any metaphysical theory as regressive in human thought. Medieval man believed that the unseen metaphysical reality was fundamental and that the physical world of reality was simply an extension or expression of the underlying metaphysical reality. This conception tended toward superstition in human thought. The Enlightenment turned this around by placing the emphasis on the physical reality. As a result, the heirs of the Enlightenment in the modern world have eliminated the metaphysical realm and the superstitions associated with it, and believe that what is nonphysical and intangible is merely the values ascribed to physical functions. So "love," for example, denotes a quality or value that man places upon a particular set of relationships. And thought, personality, or spirit in man is simply the function of the brain. But the space-free and time-free ESP phenomena suggest that there is a metaphysical order of reality. However, one should not conceive of this metaphysical reality as a regression to the medieval metaphysic. The new metaphysic, when it is fully formed, will be as different from the medieval metaphysic as modern chemistry is from alchemy. It remains true that the categories of ESP, in particular, precognition, do suggest some metaphysical construction.

My own perception of this metaphysical reality follows the lines suggested by Christian teachings. This is my personal belief, and I recognize that it is a "belief," not a "fact." I remain open to the formulation of a new metaphysic, firmly convinced that there is such a metaphysical reality but awaiting some more definitive evidence before I alter the perceptions of this reality which have been formed by my religious training.

One aspect of my religious "faith" that I hold with greater conviction because of my inquiry into parapsychology is a belief in prayer. There are at least three ways people may conceptualize prayer. One is that personal prayer and meditation are an opportunity for reflection when a person may organize his thoughts and concerns and make decisions about what he should do. Public prayer may serve the same function of stimulating reflective thought that helps a person to formulate plans for his life. Certainly prayer can serve this function for people. All persons need quiet times to collect their thoughts and think intensively about their concerns. However, if this is the only way prayer functions, then the phenomenon of prayer is psychological rather than parapsychological. Prayer becomes, along with all thought, a function of the brain, and there is no communication with others or with God. This conception does not imply any metaphysical construction.

A second way of viewing prayer is to say that through ESP and the other parapsychological mechanisms, prayer may have some influence upon other persons and perhaps upon events. If you accept the fact that ESP does occur, you can readily acknowledge that it does play some role in prayer. There are two ways in which the experimental work on ESP can give some limited support to prayer. The ESP experiments give solid evidence for the existence of communication apart from the recognized sensory apparatus. If prayer is effective communication, it must occur in an extrasensory fashion; therefore, ESP experiments may be used in support of prayer to the extent that they demonstrate the possibility of extrasensory communication. In addition, ESP may have a more direct relationship to one type of prayer—intercession. When a person prays for another person, it is possible that the desire expressed in prayer is communicated by ESP to the person who is the object of the prayer. That desire, perceived at a subconscious level, may have an effect in that person's experience. But if this should be the case, this phenomenon ceases to be prayer *in the traditional sense*, for no transcendental agency is operating in this situation. It is simply the good wishes and thoughts of one person communicated by extrasensory means to another person.

It is worth noting that some of the discoveries in parapsychology coincide with some of the religious teachings about prayer. Dr. Schmeidler's experiments, which showed that those who believe ESP is possible score higher on ESP experiments than those who do not believe it is possible, parallels the religious teaching that as a person's belief or faith grows, prayer will become a stronger force in his life. A parallel to prayer can be drawn, too, between the small amount of evidence relating the alpha brain waves with the ESP state and the practice of closing one's eyes, which induces the alpha rhythm. In this conception of prayer as an extrasensory phenomenon, there is action beyond the limits of one person's mind; there is some interaction between the minds of two or more persons and perhaps some interaction between human minds and events. But this view of prayer does not imply any transcendent being(s); God is not an integral part of this theory. This idea does imply some kind of metaphysical construction, but it is metaphysical only in the sense that man does not now understand it. It may well be that the laws that govern ESP are physical, and if they are physical, what is presently considered beyond the physical because of a lack of knowledge will become physical.

A third possible way to view prayer is to see it as communication with a transcendent being(s) through which paranormal powers are set in motion to influence persons and events. This is the traditional religious conception of prayer. For people who believe in God, and I include myself in this category, this is a meaningful conception of prayer. This view of prayer does imply a metaphysical dimension to reality that really transcends the natural and not one that will become physical as knowledge advances.

This chapter will differ from many of the writings about prayer. This is not a "how to" manual, which gives advice to persons who desire a more disciplined prayer life. Nor is it a chapter of prayers designed to assist in worship and personal devotional experiences. It is not designed to give a theological interpretation of prayer; nor is it a testimony to the effectiveness of prayer. Rather, it is an inquiry into the mechanism of prayer—how and why prayer works. It differs from the books on prayer that unquestioningly accept the thesis that prayer does work without exploring any reasons for this conclusion apart from the rather naïve conviction that "when I begin to pray, things begin to happen."

In the present skeptical age some people find it difficult to believe that prayer does work. In a previous time when a person's concerns were for his family and his job, when his community was small and rural, and when his knowledge was limited to the Bible, a few classical works of literature, and the practical skills he needed to live in a prescientific era, it was reasonably easy for him to conceive of a personal God who would hear and respond to prayers. But today man's vision is not so limited. Persons today are conscious of a world community of billions of people, their concerns reach from their homes to international politics, their knowledge extends over a wide range of subjects, and their vision goes all the way to the other side of the moon. The spirit of scientific inquiry no longer permits the naïve acceptance of a practice like prayer just because things happen when we pray (particularly since things happen when we don't pray, also). In a secular era, when we are conscious of a world full of people and their many concerns, and when we tend to view our world as controlled by natural forces, it becomes very difficult to conceptualize a personal God who hears and answers individual prayers. These factors have produced the neglect of prayer that is apparent even among Christian believers today.

In this chapter, I shall attempt to evaluate the small amount of experimentation that has been done in an effort to establish the effectiveness of prayer. Then I shall relate this to the three possible models for the operation of the phenomenon called prayer, which I just outlined.

EXPERIMENTS IN PRAYER

One type of prayer experiment has been conducted by Dr. William R. Parker and reported in his book, *Prayer Can Change Your Life*.[1] Dr. Parker, in his basic experiment, took people who were troubled by anxiety, tested them, and divided them into three groups. The people in one group entered psychotherapy to alleviate their problems. The people in a second group engaged in the individual practice of "random prayer" for the improvement of their psychological state. The people in a third group used what Dr. Parker termed "prayer therapy" in a quest to overcome their anxiety. Prayer therapy was a group process in which people came together regularly to pray for themselves and others in the group.

Tests conducted at the conclusion of the first experimental period revealed that for the people in psychotherapy there was a 65 percent rate of improvement. The group that used random prayers showed no improvement. The prayer-therapy group achieved the best results, a 72 percent rate of improvement.[2] Results similar to these were recorded in subsequent experiments.

If we assume that the results of Dr. Parker's experiments are accurately measured, one needs to ask what they demonstrate. Do they prove anything about prayer?

The results *could* be interpreted to suggest that prayer is ineffective. The group using random prayer showed no improvement, whereas the group using prayer therapy showed 72 percent improvement. Both groups used prayer, one successfully and one unsuccessfully. The variable between these two groups was that in one group, prayer was an individual experience, whereas in the other, it was a group process. This suggests one of two things: the success of prayer-therapy groups was the result of group process; or prayer, to be effective, must be a group, not an individual, activity. If Dr. Parker wanted to prove that prayer really can change one's life, he would have to add at least one more group to the experimental design, a group of people who engaged in regular group meetings and discussions about their anxieties without engaging in prayer. If this group showed a rate of improvement similar to the prayer-therapy group, Dr. Parker should change the title of his book to "Group Therapy Can Change Your Life." Dr. Parker's experiments really do not prove anything about prayer. The only conclusion one can draw from them is that a group activity, which included prayer as a medium of expression, proved about as effective as psychotherapy in helping people to handle their anxiety. The failure of the random-prayer group to show any improvement suggests that the success of the prayer-therapy group came in spite of, not because of, prayer.

Most of the experiments with prayer that are significant have involved prayer for plants. Plants are used because their growth may be measured accurately and because the other influences affecting their growth can be controlled and kept constant. In an experiment with plants, the experimental and the control groups can be given the same atmosphere, the same light, and the same amount of water, making prayer the only variable condition in the experiment. Some of the more sophisticated experimental designs with plants relate more directly to spiritual healing than to prayer, and they will appear in the next chapter. However, experiments on the effect of prayer on plants have been conducted by Franklin Loehr and are reported in his book *The Power of Prayer on Plants*.[3]

Mr. Loehr's experiments demonstrate the positive effect that prayer may have on the growth of plants. The first experiments Mr. Loehr conducted involved prayer over the water used for certain plants. A group of people gathered and directed prayers to a jar of water; then they passed the jar from person to person, and each individual gave it a personal prayer. The next day Mr. Loehr prepared six pans for planting, putting corn in two, lima beans in two, and sweet peas in two. An equal number of seeds, eight, were put in each pan, and all external conditions were kept the same. Three pans, each with one of the three kinds of seeds, were watered from a container of water that had received no prayer, whereas the other three pans were watered with an equal amount of water from the prayed-for container. The results of these tests were that seven corn plants grew in the prayed-for pan and only three in the other pan, four lima beans grew in the prayed-for pan and none in the other, and one sweet pea grew in the prayed-for pan and three in the other.[4] The final results showed the favorable influence of prayer in two of the three cases. Some further experiments using this method were even more successful.

Another method Mr. Loehr and his associates used was to pray directly for the plants. Using this design, he and his associates discovered that prayer not only could stimulate but also could inhibit growth. A couple, Mr. and Mrs. Prust, cut six slips of ivy of equal length from leafage on their backyard fence. They put three slips in one pot and three in another. Then Mr. Prust began the prayer work, directing prayers for growth at three of them and prayers for non-growth at the other three. All other conditions were kept the same. All six slips of ivy took root and began to grow. At the end of the first week there was little apparent difference in the six plants, but after two weeks there was a difference. The growth-prayer plants were thriving, but the non-growth-prayer plants were beginning to droop. Mr. Prust continued the experiment for five weeks. At this time the three growth-prayer plants were still growing well, but the three non-growth-prayer plants were dead.[5] An experiment similar in design was done with corn, and the results were equally convincing.[6]

The experiments Mr. Loehr conducted were not conclusive in their results, but they do indicate that to some degree prayer can stimulate the growth of plants. One experiment Mr. Loehr conducted involved nine prayer-circle members who prayed for corn and wheat seeds. About the same number of seeds germinated in both the prayer and the non-prayer groups, but in the case of both the corn and the wheat, the prayer seeds outgrew the non-prayer seeds by slightly more than 26 percent.[7]

Some persons had better results than others. A Mrs. Hazen in one experiment induced a positive 52.71 percent total growth advantage for prayer seedlings.[8] From these experiments Mr. Loehr stated three conclusions. First, he concluded that prayer can make a difference in the speed of germination and in the rate and vigor of plant growth. Secondly, prayer is an objective energy of some sort. Thirdly, scientific laboratory research can be done in religious fields.[9]

Mr. Loehr, in his zeal to make his point, may be guilty of an overstatement in his conclusion. His experiments do confirm the first statement in the conclusion. But the second statement is an assumption: there is no proof that prayer is an energy, particularly if "energy" is defined as a physical force. No physical force like electricity or light has been identified or measured in these experiments. The third statement is self-evident, since Mr. Loehr has conducted some experiments in prayer, but his conclusion implies that other areas of religious experience may be the subject of experimentation, and nothing in this experiment can support that implication.

But the real question that arises from these experiments is, What is prayer? Mr. Loehr raises this question: Is prayer simply a conscious act of the human mind, or is it the setting into motion of forces that represent a power (God) beyond our own? He records one experiment that gives a clue to an answer for this question, but no real proof.

Mrs. Ruth Weddle, a Los Angeles housewife, was doing a prayer-plant experiment under my direction. She was not getting much in the way of results. Then she got an idea. Her mother had died thirty-eight years before, when Ruth was about three, and Ruth had been given her mother's Bible. "My mother has always seemed close to me," she said, "especially when I use her Bible." Her father, a farmer, who had loved and prayed over his crops, had been dead some five or six years. Ruth, all on her own, decided to ask her mother and father for help with her experiment.

Carefully she planted the two pans of seeds as before.

Then she put her mother's Bible at one end of a high shelf in the closet and placed one pan of seeds on it. The other pan she put in the same closet on the same shelf, but at the opposite end. Then without going near the shelf herself, for four days she prayed for the seeds on the Bible and asked her mother and father to help them grow, too. They grew more than double the no-prayer seeds! But when she went back just to praying herself, she again got no unusual results with the plants.[10]

This experiment is not conclusive for two reasons: first, it is possible that this one time Ruth's prayers "worked" as they had not done on other occasions; secondly, it is possible that her mother's Bible could carry some force, as did the prayed-for water in other experiments, which stimulated plant growth. Nevertheless, the experiment is interesting, even if it is inconclusive.

However, another statement Mr. Loehr makes in his book seems to support the idea that prayer, at least in some of its forms, is not a force from beyond ourselves. He relates that many times experimenters got definite results with plants simply by loving them. They did not direct thoughts at them, nor did they invoke a transcendental power to help them. The sharing of one's self in love with the objects of prayer produced results.[11] This comment is supported by the experimental work done by Cleve Backster, which was reported in the previous chapter. Mr. Backster's conclusion from his experiments with the polygraph on plants is that in all levels of life in the natural world, there is some perception that occurs that does not utilize any sensory apparatus now identified. It seems quite possible that the "prayer" that was the basis for the prayer-plant experiments is simply a natural phenomenon in which good thoughts communicated by ESP provide for certain plants a more favorable atmosphere that stimulates their growth.

I conducted my own experiment following the procedure Mr. Loehr and his associates used to test his results. I planted three trays with thirty grass seeds in each one. One was the control; one I prayed for each day; and the third I watered with water that had been prayed over each day. Each tray received the same amount of water, sunshine, and heat. My experiment confirmed one part of Mr. Loehr's experiments but not another. The grass seeds in the prayed-for tray did grow better than those in the control tray. But the seeds in the tray that received the treated water did not do quite so well as those in the control tray. I kept accurate records for ten days, from day eleven to twenty. On day eleven 25 of the 26 seeds, which eventually germinated in the prayed-for tray, had already sent up their shoots. This compared with 23 of 26 in the treated-water tray and 21 of 24 in the control tray. The prayer may have had the effect of influencing an earlier germination of the seeds in the prayed-for tray. In addition, on each day, from day eleven to day twenty, I measured each shoot of grass, computing the total length of all the foliage and the average height of each plant. The prayed-for plants in those ten days grew four inches more than the control-tray plants with an average growth of one eighth inch more per plant. The increase in total growth for the treated-water plants over the same period of time was about two inches less than the control-tray plants. My experiment is not sufficiently extensive to be conclusive, but it does point in the same direction as Mr. Loehr's experiments concerning one aspect of the effect of prayer on plants, that is, direct prayer for the plants. However, it did not support Mr. Loehr's experiments involving praying over the water used for the plants. In the next chapter there will be a record of additional experiments in which water is "treated" by people who seem to be gifted as healers, which is similar to the treated-water aspect of these experiments.

It seems from this evidence that prayer may have a positive effect on plants, and presumably on people. The question that remains involves the character and dynamics of prayer. Is prayer a force within and between persons or is it a force that, at least sometimes, comes from beyond persons? No conclusive answer to this question may be drawn from these experiments.

PRAYER AND MYSTICISM

Another foray into the subject of prayer to gain some additional understanding may be made through mysticism. The technique employed in mysticism is meditation, a kind of freeing of the mind so that it may touch what is ultimate in the universe. The mystic spends time in refining techniques to accomplish this. The Christian mystic believes that in his meditation he has made contact with God, who reveals himself and his will. Evelyn Underhill has written that there are two distinct methods that people have used to get in touch with the unseen—mysticism and magic. She distinguishes between the two by saying that magic wants to get, whereas mysticism wants to give.[12] Magic, as a method, does not employ the rigorous discipline of mysticism, and it uses superstition in an attempt to captivate adherents. The two—mysticism and magic—should not be confused; yet in popular thought mysticism sometimes blurs into magic. The religious person sometimes attempts to bring the powers of the universe under control for his own use. However, though religion sometimes exhibits aspects of magic, the role that religion is expected to play in life relates to mysticism—making oneself available for service to the Ultimate Power of the universe.

Mysticism exists in some form in most of the religions of the world. One of its basic views is the division of the world into appearance and reality. Different words are used in different systems to distinguish these, but the principle remains the same. The world that men see as they live is the world of appearance. It is passing and impermanent. It never remains the same. But beyond this world of appearance is reality, which is permanent, stable, never-changing. Some of the pairs of words used to distinguish the two are temporal and eternal, immanent and transcendent, human and divine. The unseen reality the mystic seeks may be named God, Ultimate Reality, Pure Being, Spirit, or some other abstract term. This unseen reality is difficult to define or describe, but it is accepted by mystics as that which is authentic and true in human existence.

The path the mystic takes to reach this unseen reality involves blotting out the temporal world in an effort to concentrate on ultimate reality. Different mystics have used different schemes to measure the progress along this way. William R. Inge, in his classic work *Christian Mysticism*, sets forth three stages along the way.[13] The first stage he calls the purgative life, which includes contrition, confession, and self-discipline. The second stage is called the illuminative life, and in it the mystic concentrates his will, intellect, and feeling upon God and upon willingly, even spontaneously, performing the good works of God. The last stage in the mystic's journey is the unitive or contemplative life, in which man beholds God face to face and is united with him. The final stage is, of course, the most difficult to attain. There are certain conditions and methods that help—quiet and concentration on some symbol or thought—but the mystic must practice this regularly and over a long period of time to reach the unitive experience. When the Christian mystic feels a sense of unity with God, then he has some sense of communication through visions or imagination with God and his purpose. When a person has a glimpse of this reality, then he attempts to purify himself by getting rid of illusion, evil, and imperfections, that are not in harmony with this view of reality.

The mystic in some other religions, Zen Buddhism, particularly, does not search for the reality beyond, but for the reality within. D. T. Suzuki, who is one of the foremost interpreters of Zen Buddhism to the Western world, identifies the basic idea of Zen as enabling a person to come in contact with the inner workings of his own being.[14] Zen rejects all external authority and places absolute faith in one's inner being. This inner being is beyond the senses and the intellect of a person; it is beyond knowledge and logic. To wander in the domain of the senses and intellect is to pursue the shadow or the ego. The real ego is somewhere else, and it must be caught not from outside but from within.[15] The catching of the ego from within is the enlightenment experience, which involves seeing things from a higher point of understanding so that everything in life may be arranged where it properly belongs. This enables a person to order his life according to the wisdom he gains in meditation.

In this cursory survey of mysticism, the problem that arose in the previous section arises again. That there is a mystical experience one cannot deny. It has been a very meaningful experience for some people, an experience that has motivated them to do acts that are loving and good. But what is the dynamic in this experience? Is it communication with God, who is beyond man, as the Christian mystic would affirm, or is it communication within one's self, as the Buddhists believe? There is no experiment or experience coming from mysticism that can affirm conclusively one or the other.

One interesting precognition experiment reported in Chapter 2 suggests that a person may have communication with some idea structure beyond himself. The experiment was one conducted by John Mihalasky and E. Douglas Dean. They were testing to see if extrasensory perception, specifically precognition, was a factor in successful management decisions.

Since the higher the organizational level of the decision maker, the more his decisions are based on imperfect data and deal with the future, John Mihalasky in his experiments tested groups of executives in the upper levels of their business organizations. A test first divided the men into dynamic and nondynamic personality types. Then those participating in the experiment were told to guess the individual values of a 100 digit number, which was to be generated for them in the future. The digits were punched on an IBM computer randomly producing a 100 digit number, and then that number was compared digit by digit, with the column-by-column guesses punched into the participant's cards. The hypothesis tested was that dynamic men would score higher than nondynamic men in this precognition test. In sixteen of twenty experiments this proved correct. In all the experiments with nearly a thousand participants, the dynamic men scored 11.08 percent correct guesses whereas the nondynamic men scored 9.52 percent, where the chance level was 10 percent.[16]

An analysis of these twenty experiments showed the relation of tenure of office as chief operating officer of the company to the company's profit trend over the preceding five years. A correlation between precognition scores and profit patterns indicated that all executives who increased their company's profits by more than 100 percent in that time period scored above chance.[17] The experimenters do not draw any conclusions from this except to say that precognition tests should be used as an additional tool for the selection of top executives. However, the results seem to indicate that certain people are able successfully to draw upon a structure of ideas or thoughts beyond them that may help them in their decision-making process.

Precognition, as was noted at the beginning of this chapter, is the most difficult of all paranormal activities to explain without some reference to a being beyond human experience. If a person can perceive the future before it occurs, one of three conditions may exist. The human brain may be able to gather data by extrasensory means and correctly interpret it subconsciously; time may be an illusion, making all events contemporaneous at some plane of existence; or there may be some being(s) beyond man who, because he has a better vantage point, may more accurately see the future. My personal feeling is that the third theory is most plausible; this is the one I accept.

But whichever of the three theories one holds, prayer and meditation have some application to life. For example, if executives are able to draw information of a precognitive nature from some source beyond them, is it not possible that all people potentially possess this ability to a degree? Perhaps some meditative techniques may facilitate this process. No conclusive fact may be drawn from this, but certainly there is here the suggestion that the possibility of extrasensory perception between an unseen mind encompassing a structure of ideas and a human being can exist. This tends to confirm the belief that a person may receive guidance from beyond himself through prayer.

But can we call that unseen mind with a structure of ideas "God"? Certainly there is no proof here of the traditional view of God. There is only an indication that prayer and meditation may be useful techniques in helping to make decisions dealing with the future.

Summary

It is apparent from the rather meager data in this chapter that in "prayer" there may be effective extrasensory communication that can be helpful to a person. Of the three models for the dynamic of prayer stated earlier in the chapter, the experimental evidence seems to indicate that prayer is more than just reflective thought. There seems to be some kind of extrasensory communication operating in the prayer experience. But the question remains, Is prayer simply extrasensory perception between persons, or does it involve some being(s) who is unseen?

One may construct two models for the dynamic of prayer. The one model views prayer as a type of extrasensory perception. When a person prays, he is simply projecting good thoughts which may be helpful for another person. When he meditates, he picks up thoughts that are "in the air" and uses them as a basis for his decisions. There is no being, God or anyone else, beyond him, hearing what he says or revealing anything in response. Prayers of adoration, thanksgiving, and confession to a deity simply have psychological value for a person. Prayers of petition, insofar as someone else is necessary to fulfill a petition, may be effective. Prayers of intercession, which really become in this model good thoughts projected to another person, do have value. In addition, meditation, which is drawing upon some structure of ideas, may help a person in his decision-making.

The other model for prayer is more traditional. An unseen being(s) exists who transcends the normal level of human experience. In prayer and meditation there is effective communication between a person and this being(s). Prayers of thanksgiving have the same meaning between a person and a transcendental being as words of thanksgiving between persons. Prayers of confession result in a feeling of forgiveness communicated from beyond man. In prayers of petition the being in the transcendental level may assist in granting the desires of the person praying if these desires are good for him. In prayers of intercession the transcendental being responds to the prayer by ministering to the needs of the prayed-for person. In this model there is the dynamic interaction between the immanent and transcendental spheres.

These two models for prayer may not be mutually exclusive. Some elements of both may operate in the prayer experience. For example, in prayers of intercession the person who is the object of a prayer may receive help from the good thoughts communicated by ESP from the person praying; in addition, the prayer may prompt a spiritual being to minister spiritually to that person with his good thoughts and actions. This is the personal conclusion that I have adopted from this study.

The whole issue of whether one believes that prayer puts in motion forces that come from beyond man hinges on one's belief about a transcendental spiritual realm. If such a sphere of activity does exist, it is possible that prayer does utilize power from beyond man.

The conclusion of this study on prayer includes statements on two levels of certainty. The first one, which has a higher degree of certainty, is that prayer is an effective type of communication that may create a more favorable situation for both the praying and the prayed-for person.

The second statement, which cannot be set forth with as high a degree of certainty, is that prayer puts in motion spiritual forces beyond men, which operate to make the prayer effective.

These statements have an application to the ministry of the church. The admonition heard in the church today that we don't need prayers, we need action, may be a helpful correction against the attitude that everything can be accomplished by prayer alone. But the implication of this statement is that prayer has no value in human experience. It is more correct to say we need prayer *and* action in the church. Prayer has a legitimate function in the ministry of the church; it is not so irrelevant as some people believe.

Prayer, which is communication between God and man, is central in the worship experience. If prayer is effective, then worship is an experience in which man contacts powers and forces beyond himself. This validates worship, prayer, and spiritual devotion, making this aspect of the church's ministry meaningful. Action should not be a substitute for prayer any more than prayer should be a substitute for action. Both have a role in the ministry of the church; and in that ministry there should be a dynamic and vital balance between the two.

4

SPIRITUAL HEALING

A prominent part of the ministry of Jesus reported in the Gospels was the healing of people who were ill. The four Gospels record twenty-six cases of individual healings by Jesus and ten instances when he healed larger numbers of people.[1] His followers viewed the healing of disease not as an incidental part of his work, but as an integral part of his ministry of redemption. They saw his healings as an affirmative symbol that Jesus had power over the evil forces in the universe.

The ability to heal diseases was reported, too, among the followers of Jesus. The Lord commissioned the seventy whom he sent out to heal those who were ill. The Acts of the Apostles records sixteen incidents in which the followers of Jesus healed people.[2]

If healing was such an important part of the recorded ministries of Jesus and his early followers, why does it not play a prominent role in the ministry of the church today? People have answered this question in different ways. One explanation that is offered is that the healing ministry is not strong in the church today because the church has deviated from the dependence on the power of the Holy Spirit, which was so much in evidence at the beginning. As the church early in its history became embroiled in theological discussions and controversies and in organizational concerns, it lost its dependence on the direct inspiration of the Holy Spirit. As a result, its faith diminished and the power of healing declined.[3] A second explanation is that the healing miracles of Jesus were signs of divine compassion for people, which Jesus was able to perform because he was a unique person.[4] Healings like those Jesus performed, then, are not repeatable events because there has never been another person like him. People cannot expect to duplicate Jesus' miracles because they do not possess his divine power, runs this argument. Jesus utilized some techniques, such as forgiveness and suggestion, that people may use to aid the healing process, but for the most part they must depend on the natural treatments and techniques of medicine that have been provided by God for the healing of disease. This theory, however, does not explain the healing miracles performed by the disciples of Jesus after his death, for they were not unique persons in the same sense that Jesus was.

A third possibility sometimes presented to explain the lack of a powerful healing ministry in the church today is that in the prescientific age in which Jesus lived, he and others were able to effect healings by suggestion on persons who suffered from psychogenic ailments, that is, illness in which physical symptoms develop from psychological rather than from organic disorders. The stories of miraculous healings in the Gospels, some persons say, are exaggerated and enhanced so that Jesus' actual ability as a healer was not so great as the records indicate. Furthermore, those who claim to cure people today by faith-healing techniques do only what Jesus did; that is, by offering forgiveness and assurance they effect a "cure" of those illnesses that have only a psychological cause.

One other possible explanation for Jesus' healing miracles is that the reported miracles are a mythology developed by his followers between the time of his death and the recording of the events of his life. These stories had symbolic elements in them that were interpreted by people of his day as signs of his power. There was, then, no more "spiritual" healing in Jesus' day than there is in our day. The reports of his healing miracles are mythological constructions designed to communicate truth that is symbolic rather than factual.

In the context of these theories about Jesus' healing and faith healing, one must examine the claims of those who profess to heal disease by spiritual means. Most Christian faith healers accept some form of the first theory. They believe that healing takes place through the power of the Holy Spirit, and as people trust this power more fully, healing becomes more possible. In this chapter I shall first relate some observations I have made in healing services and some evidence I have gathered concerning claims of success in healing. Then I shall discuss the relation of psychosomatic medicine to spiritual healing. In the final section, before the conclusion, I shall review some experiments that have demonstrated a power or energy some people seem to generate that may have a healing effect.

The Work of Spiritual Healing

Kathryn Kuhlman began her healing ministry nearly twenty-five years ago in Franklin, Pennsylvania. Today many people who have witnessed her work believe that she is the greatest charismatic personality in the church. She conducts regular healing services in Pittsburgh and Los Angeles and travels all over the country to conduct healing missions. She has a regular radio and television program and has published several books. Miss Kuhlman shuns denominational labels, but her approach is strongly Pentecostal and her greatest support comes from this segment of the church.

I attended a Kathryn Kuhlman service at the Washington convention of the Full Gospel Business Men's Fellowship International held in the ballroom of the Washington Hilton Hotel in February, 1970. Several thousand people filled the ballroom for this service. Miss Kuhlman appeared in a brightly colored gown; her presentation was dramatic and polished. She spoke for nearly an hour about some experiences she had had in a visit to Vietnam and some healing incidents that had taken place there. Then, rather abruptly, she changed her theme to the work of the Holy Spirit. Following this, she led everyone in prayer for the coming of the Spirit. After saying several times that she could strongly sense the power of the Spirit, the healings began.

Miss Kuhlman's technique is so extraordinary that it is nearly incredible. She will point into one section of the crowd and say, "A woman out there is being healed of arthritis." Then, as the woman stands up and swings her formerly afflicted arm over her head, an usher will lead her to the platform. By this time Miss Kuhlman has indicated others who are being healed. As the people come to the platform, she places her hands on them, and they fall over. Miss Kuhlman claims that this is the power of the Holy Spirit "hitting" them. Those who experience this say that the force is overwhelming, and they actually black out because of it. I could hardly believe what I was seeing.

From that crowd of several thousand, I saw some hundred people who claimed to be healed. Quite a number of healings were for arthritis. The people swung their arms high over their heads without pain and claimed they had been unable to do this for years. Two men suffering from arthritis of the spine were able to touch their toes when moments before, they claimed, they could not bend at all without excruciating pain. One person who had been partially paralyzed by a stroke showed no evidence of paralysis after the healing. A woman, Miss Kuhlman said, had been healed of cancer. A girl who had been deaf in one ear from birth claimed to hear through this ear, and a person who had had an unsuccessful operation to restore her hearing was healed. Another person who said she could not move her head without pain after her neck had been injured in an accident was healed, and a woman whose hand had been crippled since she was eight years old demonstrated how her hand had been straightened and freed. There were numerous other claims of healing. Of course, in this service no medical records from before and after the healings were presented to substantiate the claims that were made. But the entire demonstration was quite convincing.

Miss Kuhlman, in her book *I Believe in Miracles*,[5] gives the records of a number of healings that have taken place in her meetings. Many of these records do contain the medical data from before and after to confirm that healings indeed occurred. These healings include a lady who had cancer that had spread so far that doctors gave her only six to eight weeks to live, a man whose one eye had been blinded in an industrial accident twenty years before, a man with emphysema, a dope addict, an alcoholic, a woman with heart disease, and a man crippled from war injuries. Are these claims of healing modern-day miracles, as Miss Kuhlman says? Allen Spraggett, a minister who is the religious news editor of the *Toronto Star* and a respected psychic investigator, has spent some time investigating the claims of people who say they have been healed in Kathryn Kuhlman meetings. In a book he has written on Miss Kuhlman, he testifies that after examining the medical records of some people who had been healed, he was convinced that the claims were authentic. Kathryn Kuhlman's miracles are just that— miracles, reports Mr. Spraggett.[6]

I have received additional evidence for the authenticity of the healings at Miss Kuhlman's meetings through personal reports from members of a group with which I was affiliated. Some members of this group attended a Kuhlman meeting in Pittsburgh. Healings occurred in several people in the group, including a man who had a severe heart condition. These healings were verified by doctors who had examined the people before and after they attended the Kuhlman service. This accumulated evidence from different sources supports the claim that actual healings do occur in Kathryn Kuhlman's meetings.

The healing services conducted by Olga and Ambrose Worrall are quite different from Miss Kuhlman's services. Mr. and Mrs. Worrall both possess psychic gifts, and they have devoted much of their lives to healing people. They conduct a New Life Clinic, which is held every Thursday morning at the Mt. Washington Methodist Church in Baltimore, Maryland. The meeting starts at 10 A.M., and for the first thirty or forty minutes Mrs. Worrall or one of the two men, a minister and a layman who assist her, speak to the group about healing. Then from 10:40 to 11 A.M. there is silence in the sanctuary as people spiritually prepare themselves for the healing service. At 11 A.M. a simple service begins with a hymn, a prayer, and a short meditation. Then Mrs. Worrall and her associates approach the altar rail, and those who desire to be healed come to kneel there. After speaking briefly and quietly with each one to learn what ailment he has, they lay their hands on the person and pray. In the services I have attended, between fifty and eighty people have come forward for prayer. The Worralls report that many healings have resulted in these services. These healings, they say, cover every range of illness. Some of them are psychosomatic illnesses in which the symptoms are real but have a psychological origin. Some are functional in which the illness is real but has a psychological cause. And many are organic, proved, and diagnosed by medical tests.[7] Some healings have occurred right at the altar whereas others have occurred gradually over a period of time. The services the Worralls conduct are much less dramatic and spectacular than are Miss Kuhlman's services. There are no testimonials, no emotional outbursts, and no displays of healing. Everything occurs in a very quiet and meditative atmosphere. Yet apparently they are as successful.

Another aspect of the Worrall's healing ministry takes place in their home, where on occasion people come to receive Mr. Worrall's ministrations. In a "healing room" in the home he meditates and lays his hands on the afflicted person. In addition, regularly each evening at 9 o'clock the Worralls and all who are interested in their works pause, where they are, to pray for the healing of people. I personally know of two situations in which persons have been healed by Mr. and Mrs. Worrall. One is a lady who suffered for many years from arthritis of the spine. She had received medical treatment throughout this time, but her back became quite crippled and painful. Mr. and Mrs. Worrall were visiting her church for an evening program. When Mr. Worrall noticed her condition, he put his hand on her back and said, "You have a good back." She was ready to disagree with him when she realized he wanted her to believe she had a good back. At home that night she noticed that her back was straighter and that the pain was gone. She has not been troubled by the arthritis since that evening.

A second healing of which I have knowledge involves a girl who was to have surgery to remove a growth on her neck. Although this growth was not a serious disorder, it was uncomfortable and unsightly. Before surgery took place, she went to one of Mrs. Worrall's healing services. After that service in which she received Mrs. Worrall's ministrations, the growth began to diminish in size, and several weeks later it had completely disappeared. In addition to these instances of healing, there are some case histories, with the medical verification of healings, contained in Mr. and Mrs. Worrall's book.[8] Included in these is a letter from a doctor, verifying the healing of a woman from a cancerous tumor. There is good evidence that healing does take place in the Worralls' services.

Another person who is well known in some circles for his healing services is the Reverend Alfred W. Price, rector of St. Stephen's Episcopal Church in Philadelphia. Dr. Price conducted a healing mission in Annapolis, Maryland, which I attended. His healing service followed the order for worship in *The Book of Common Prayer*. At the time of the prayers people came to the altar rail to receive the laying on of hands and prayers for healing. Dr. Price conducts similar services at St. Stephen's each Thursday. A part of his healing ministry is a Prayer Fellowship which includes about 135 people who have committed themselves to a discipline of intercessory prayer. They follow a schedule so that each moment of every day and night at least one of them is offering prayer for healing for persons on their prayer list. Dr. Price has published a booklet containing the testimonies of those who have been healed through this ministry. There are letters that testify to healing from alcoholism, asthma, a brain tumor, blindness, cancer, diabetes, encephalitis, heart disease, multiple sclerosis, and many other diseases. Dr. Price's reputation is well established among responsible people in his church and community, and this also testifies to the effectiveness of his ministry.

I am including with the material in this chapter an account of a healing ministry that I have not personally investigated. This is the well-known ministry at the Healing Shrine of Lourdes, France. This Roman Catholic shrine was established over a century ago when a young girl, Bernadette, had a series of visions of a figure purported to be the Virgin Mary. In the sixth vision the apparition instructed Bernadette to drink at a fountain and wash there. She scratched away some sand at the place indicated, and a spring of water came forth. The water from this spring is believed to have healing powers, and thousands of people come to Lourdes each year to be healed. A Medical Bureau at Lourdes assesses carefully every claim of healing. This Bureau has compiled an account of sixty-two cures that can be proved by medical records.[9] Dr. John Sutherland Bonnell reports on his visit to Lourdes in a recent book he has written. He believes that a considerable number of people in addition to these sixty-two have been healed, but their healings are not recorded officially because their medical records are incomplete.[10] Even so, there are very few cures when one considers the millions who have visited the shrine in the past hundred years. Dr. Bonnell reports the statement of the medical director at Lourdes, who said that every year approximately 300,000 baths are taken in the healing waters, but on the average only forty persons of that total make any claim of being cured. Of these forty there may be only one who would be certified by the medical committee as a verified healing.[11] One reason there are so few recognized cures is that Pope Benedict XIV laid down stringent requirements for recognition of cures. Some of these requirements are that the malady must be organic and not functional, that the healing must be instantaneous and not progressive, that it must have all the elements of permanency (no case is authenticated unless four to six years of medical supervision has followed the cure), that a cure must not be claimed if any medication that could at least partially account for it had been administered, that the cure must not only be spontaneous, but complete, and that there must be no regression in the patient's condition.[12] Because the medical bureau is so thorough in its judgment, one can be reasonably certain that the sixty-two healings are really instances of healings that have no medical explanation.

This survey of the results of these healing ministries tends to verify the claim that healing may take place through spiritual means. In addition, it reveals that a variety of techniques and styles may be used by people to achieve results. Further investigation, then, should focus not on discovering any particular method for spiritual healing but on exploring some possible reasons why such healing occurs.

PSYCHOSOMATIC MEDICINE

Until fairly recent decades the medical viewpoint on disease was that illness was caused by an organic cellular disturbance; that is, every disturbed function (illness) is the result of a disturbed structure. Following this reasoning, a heart ailment results from cellular deterioration in the heart muscle; in this etiological pattern the cellular disease that is a structural deterioration produces the condition in the heart muscle that causes the physiological disturbance. This theory is that disease has an organic origin. Early in this century, however, some doctors discovered that certain ailments seemed to follow a different causative pattern. In this pattern a disturbed function is the cause rather than the result of the structural alteration that creates the physiological disturbance. For example, tension (a disturbed function) may cause vaso-constriction, which in turn makes the heart work harder, which causes structural alteration, which causes a physiological disturbance. Perhaps a better example is the causative chain that results in peptic ulcers: emotional factors cause a chronic gastric condition, which results in peptic ulcers. This causative chain leads to an illness that may be functional. The disease is caused by the continuous functional stress that arises for an individual in his daily living. Therefore, fear, aggression, guilt, and frustration, if repressed, may result in permanent chronic emotional tensions that disturb the functions of certain body organs, especially those organs which have to do with digestion, respiration, and circulation.[13]

There is much evidence to support this functional theory. Emotional factors seem to make a person more susceptible to disease. It has been demonstrated conclusively that the relationship between mind and body is such that a person's emotional or mental state will cause physiological change. There is the obvious effect of embarrassment producing blushing, and anger affecting blood pressure. There are also the examples of chronic functional disturbances producing physical illness, as is true in the case of a peptic ulcer. It has been adequately demonstrated, too, that the "will to live" is a factor in recovery from illness. In addition, psychological and emotional conditions have been demonstrated as causative factors in many kinds of illness.

So far I have mentioned two kinds of illnesses—organic illness in which cellular disease causes a physical disturbance and functional illness in which emotional factors cause cellular disease which causes a physical disturbance. There is yet another category of illness—psychogenic ailments. These illnesses have a psychological origin. For example, the fear of cancer may produce the symptoms of cancer although the cellular disease which may be diagnosed as cancer is absent. A person may unconsciously create the symptoms of a disease because of his psychological or emotional condition. The popular way of describing this is that a person "imagines" he is ill.

A medical textbook on psychosomatic medicine suggests that about a third of the people who consult a physician have no definite bodily disease to account for their illness. Their illness is psychogenic. Another third of the patients a doctor sees have symptoms that in part depend on emotional factors, but organic findings are present. Their illness is functional. A final third of the patients coming to a physician are suffering from organic illness.[14] The important point to note is that psychosomatic factors may have an effect upon all three categories of illness. Even in the case of organic illness, the psychological factor may be very important in the management of the disease.

Is it possible now to use this psychosomatic factor in illness to explain what happens in spiritual healing? For psychogenic ailments the answer is obvious. Here the illness is not organic; the pattern of symptoms exists only in the mind of a person, and it persists there because of some psychological need or condition that affects that person. The spiritual healer deals with this psychological condition as he instills confidence to overcome fear or offers forgiveness to overcome guilt. When the psychological state of the person is transformed, the symptoms disappear and the person is "healed." But should this be called "healing"? It is true that a person who experiences this change can now function better in his social situation, but no organic healing takes place. Some critics of spiritual healers say that the success of healers is confined to psychogenic illnesses, that they do not really heal organic disease; yet the evidence presented in the previous section reveals that in some instances of spiritual healing organic change apparently does take place.

In the category of functional illness in which emotions are a factor in causing the structural change related to disease, it is possible that a spiritual healer, by offering faith, confidence, forgiveness, peace, or some other supportive and constructive feeling to alter a person's emotional state, may remove the emotional disturbance that caused the organic change. With the change in the emotional state the cellular damage caused by the destructive emotion begins to be repaired by the natural healing forces in the body. This is both a plausible and probable explanation for many healings that occur by spiritual means. Here spiritual factors that have inhibited the natural healing forces of the body are removed, and the body begins to heal itself.

The one question that remains is: Can organic disease be cured by spiritual means? Can spiritual forces affect disease that is purely physical? Three possibilities exist here. One is that spiritual forces can have no effect on such disease. Another is that spiritual healers can help a person with organic disease to manage his illness better. In other words, the illness is not healed, but the person's attitude is changed so that he can better cope with it. The other possibility is that spiritual forces can heal organic disease. It is difficult to give a conclusive response to the question because doctors cannot determine accurately when a disease is totally organic. But there *is* evidence that suggests that organic disease can be healed by spiritual means.

EXPERIMENTS WITH HEALING HANDS

Several experiments that tend to confirm that the laying on of hands may have a healing effect have been conducted by Dr. Bernard Grad, a McGill University biochemist. The results of these experiments indicate that there may be a force in the hands of some persons that can be described as a healing power. I will report on three of Dr. Grad's experiments and on some additional experiments by Sister M. Justa Smith, Ph.D., of Rosary Hill College in Buffalo, which build on Dr. Grad's work. Dr. Grad and Sister Justa work with the same healer in their recorded experiments, Oskar Estebany, a retired Hungarian army colonel.

The first experiments Dr. Grad conducted were designed to investigate in a controlled experimental situation, where the operation of suggestion was unlikely, whether a healer might mediate a healing power.[15] Mice were used in the experiment. A cut of equal size was made with a surgical instrument on the back of each mouse. The mice were separated into three groups— one group was treated by the healer, one group was treated by different individuals who claimed no healing abilities, and the third group, the control group, received no treatment. Treatment consisted of holding caged mice between the hands for fifteen-minute periods twice each day. Each day through twenty days of such treatment the size of the wounds was measured in square inches. During the first ten days of treatment there was no significant difference in the size of the wounds on the three groups of mice. But by the fifteenth day a small but significant difference in the rate of healing was apparent. The control group and the group treated by various people displayed about the same healing rates, but the wounds on the group treated by Col. Estebany were healing significantly more rapidly. In one experiment on day fifteen the wounds were .028 square inches on the control group, .032 square inches on the group treated by different individuals, and .020 square inches on the group treated by Col. Estebany. On day sixteen the size of the wounds in the same order were .022 (control),

.026 (treated by different persons), and .013 (Col. Estebany's group).[16] With these results Dr. Grad concludes that this small but significant difference in the healing of animals treated by Col. Estebany may be attributed to some influence he had upon them.[17] The experiments tend to support the claim that Col. Estebany's hands had some effect on the healing process.

A second series of experiments that Dr. Grad did with Col. Estebany involved barley plants.[18] In this experiment twenty barley seeds were planted in each of a number of pots which then were divided into two equal groups. Col. Estebany held a sealed flask that contained 350 milliliters of a 1 percent aqueous sodium chloride solution between his hands for fifteen minutes. He did not come in contact with the plants themselves. Technicians poured 25 ml. of this treated water on each pot in one group, while an equal amount of tap water was poured on the pots in a second group, the control plants. Then both the treated and the untreated pots were thoroughly dried in an oven for forty-eight hours. After that, both groups of pots were watered with tap water— 25 ml. for each pot the first day and 15 ml. each second day thereafter. In all respects the two groups were treated alike. Three types of records were kept on the growth of the plants for thirteen days—number of plants, height of plants (in millimeters), and total foliage yield (in millimeters). The number of plants was not significantly different, but the height and the total yield were. The difference in average height was 22 mm. (control) to 32 mm. (treated) on day nine, 29 mm. (control) to 44 mm. (treated) on day eleven, and 36 mm. (control) to 46 mm. (treated) on day thirteen. The difference in total average yield was 251 mm. (control) to 399 mm. (treated) on day nine, 394 mm. (control) to 578 mm. (treated) on day eleven, and 486 mm. (control) to 628 mm. (treated) on day thirteen.[19]

The conclusion Dr. Grad draws from this is that Col. Estebany altered 350 ml. of a 1 percent aqueous sodium chloride solution by holding it in his hands for fifteen minutes, and this alteration was apparent in the significantly greater yield in treated plants than in the control plants.[20] This effect could not be due to any chemical substance but must be attributed to some force that passed from the hands into the water through the glass bottle.

The third study done by Dr. Grad did not involve Col. Estebany. The experiment was conducted in the same way as the one previously described except that there were four groups of plants—three treated by three different persons and one control group. The three persons were JB, a psychiatrically normal person; RH, who suffered from a neurotic depression; and HR, who was ill with a psychotic depression. The main hypothesis that the experiment was designed to test was that a solution held for thirty minutes in the hands of an individual in a stimulated, confident mood would permit plants watered by this solution to grow at a faster rate than identical solutions held for the same time by persons with a depressive illness or not held by anyone (the control group).[21] The measurements taken on the groups revealed no significant difference in number, height, and yield on days zero to ten and sixteen. The difference on days eleven, thirteen, and fourteen was of borderline significance, and the difference on days twelve and fifteen was significant. The trend in all the measurements gave JB's pots the highest value, followed by RH's, then the untreated controls, while the lowest occurred in HR's pots. The average heights of the plants on day twelve were 28 mm. for JB's plants, 23 mm. for RH's, 20 mm. for the control group, and 18 mm. for HR's. The average height on day fifteen followed the same pattern: 41 mm. for JB's, 38 mm. for RH's, 32 mm. for the control, and 29 mm. for HR's. Similar results are given for the average yield on the same days.

The results of the experiment do not confirm the hypothesis, since one would normally expect the plants watered by the solution held by RH, a neurotic depressive, to show a lower yield than the control group. However, the experimenters noticed that RH did not exhibit a depressive mood when she held the water between her hands. When she was told the purpose of the experiment, she responded with an expression of interest and a decided brightening of mood. She cradled the bottle in her lap much as a mother would hold a child. On the other hand, HR's attitude while he held the bottle was anxious, agitated, and depressed. The experiment seems to indicate that results are determined by the mood of the person at the time he treats the water. A positive mood seems to stimulate cell growth, whereas a negative mood inhibits it. This would suggest that in the ritual practice of laying on of hands for healing a positive mood may facilitate the healing effect.

Sister M. Justa Smith's experiments build on the work that Dr. Grad has done. Sister Justa received her doctoral degree for original research on the effects of ultraviolet light and of high magnetic fields upon enzyme activity. Enzymes are considered by some biochemists to be the catalysts that control metabolic reactions in cells. If this theory is correct, then disease or illness proceeds from either a lack of or a malfunctioning of an enzyme. A change in cellular structure from disease back to health would require a prior change in the catalysts—the enzymes. In Sister Justa's previous experiments she had discovered that magnetic fields increased enzyme activity, whereas ultraviolet light damaged the enzyme and decreased the activity.

Sister Justa used the same Col. Estebany in her experiments that Dr. Grad did in his. The enzyme used was trypsin. Each day during the experiments solutions of trypsin were prepared and divided into four containers. In one container the trypsin was left in its native state to serve as a control. The trypsin in the second container was treated by Col. Estebany, who placed his hands around the bottle for 75 minutes. Portions of the solution were taken out after 15, 30, 45, and 60 minutes to measure any change of activity. The trypsin in a third container was damaged by ultraviolet light and then treated by the Colonel in the same way he treated the other solution. The trypsin in the fourth container was exposed to high magnetic fields for hourly increments up to three hours.[22] The results of the experiment showed that the enzymes treated by Col. Estebany exhibited an increase in activity significantly greater than the control enzymes. The increase in activity of the enzymes in bottles held by Col. Estebany was comparable to the increase obtained in a magnetic field of 13,000 gauss (the natural magnetic field of the earth is less than one gauss). The same rate of increased activity was noted in both the damaged and the normal enzymes treated by Col. Estebany.

This enzyme study indicates that some force or energy that produces measurable change is activated by Col.

Estebany's hands. Sister Justa thinks that this may be a "field" similar to a magnetic field, which in some way may activate a power that produces healing.[23] These experiments point toward a more natural explanation for spiritual healing, although the source of this force or energy is not indicated by the experiments.

The experiments that Dr. Grad and Sister Justa have conducted demonstrate that some persons are able to effect physical change through a force or energy that is mediated through their hands. This force may be the healing power that spiritual healers convey through the laying on of hands.

CONCLUSION

The observations I have been able to make of certain spiritual healers and the small amount of medical information I have gathered on certain alleged healings indicate that healing may result from the ministrations of certain people. The experimental data from the Grad and Smith experiments point in the same direction.

Contributions to healing may come to persons by one of three means—through medicine, through altering the emotional state of a person, and through a certain force described as spiritual that is found in the hands of a "gifted" person. People described as spiritual healers may effect change through two of these three means: they may alter the emotional state of a person by offering confidence and forgiveness, or they may be the channels of a healing force. A problem here is that the actual mechanism of healing is not clear to scientists. The human body has certain natural means of attacking disease. When germs or foreign materials enter the body, or when injuries occur, these natural means of healing begin to operate. But the way this natural force is activated and the way certain medicines affect it is unknown. Doctors cannot explain, for example, how an aspirin or a tranquilizer works. It is possible, therefore, that medicine, healthy emotions, and the healing force in spiritual healing all have a positive effect upon the same bodily mechanisms, enzymes perhaps, which aid the natural healing agents in the body.

In the case of psychogenic and functional illnesses, then, a spiritual healer, as well as other persons, may be able to change the emotional state of the ill person by offering confidence, forgiveness, or some other positive emotion. In psychogenic illnesses this could cause the symptoms of the illness to disappear instantly; in functional illnesses this could initiate the gradual process of healing. The real issue, however, raised in this chapter is whether the healing force that is conveyed in the laying-on-of-hands experiments is the agent that spiritual healers use. First, what is this force? It has been demonstrated that this force or energy may effect change, but the force itself has not been described or measured. It is possible that the healing force is some form of physical energy that has not yet been defined and measured. Again, it may be a force that will always defy physical descriptions and measurements and will remain in the realm we call "spiritual." Experiments have demonstrated that this healing force may be mediated through the hands, so this force probably is the healing power given in the laying on of hands in services such as those conducted by the Worralls and by Dr. Price. But is this force also to be found in the water at Lourdes? Certainly the healing force can be contained in water; this has been demonstrated by Dr. Grad's experiments with plants. Although the water at Lourdes is not chemically different from other water, experiments have been conducted that indicate that it does possess some healing property. In these experiments animals injected with germs subjected to water from Lourdes did not develop disease, whereas similar animals injected with germs subjected to water from another river did develop disease.[24] The Lourdes water apparently had some effect on the germs. The water at Lourdes, however, is not handled by a healer. One is left with several possibilities. The healing force is placed in the water by a supernatural being, or it is put there by the prayers and devoted acts of faithful people. It is true, too, that some people are healed at Lourdes of functional disorders because the healing ritual has produced in them an emotional change. But the certified healings at Lourdes probably are the result of a healing force in the water, mediated through a spiritual being or through prayers of the faithful.

Kathryn Kuhlman's healing technique presents a slightly different problem. Here the healing force seems to be present "in the air." People apparently are healed apart from the laying on of hands or any other physical ministration. One can understand how Miss Kuhlman might effect psychogenic and functional illnesses, since her services are charged with emotion. But is a healing force actually present and operative in her services? Until this force can be more accurately described and measured, one cannot conclusively answer this question. Because of the remarkably rapid healing in her services of illness, which is medically substantiated, one tends to believe that some force beyond a positive emotional state does operate. Again there are several possibilities. One could postulate a spiritual being, the Holy Spirit, or discarnate beings as the agents of healing; or it may be that in a crowd at a service where everyone has his attention focused on healing, the healing force is generated in such a way that it radiates through the room apart from actual physical contact with a healer. Until this force can be defined and measured, each of these remains a possibility.

Perhaps at this point we should review what the evidence in this chapter suggests. First, there are significant numbers of well-documented cases in which recovery from illness cannot be explained by the best medical knowledge. In many of these cases a person who has a reputation for effecting "spiritual healing" has apparently contributed to the recovery through some nonmedical ministration. This healing may result from a "healing force" that has been demonstrated in experimental situations, and this fits in with some of the other fragmentary evidence being accumulated by parapsychologists about unidentified forces in our world.

But the healing phenomenon raises a very difficult question. Why are some people healed while others are not? I wrote earlier of persons I know who have apparently been healed through the ministrations of those who have a reputation for healing. But I know persons, too, who have gone to healing services conducted by the same "healers" and have not been healed. There apparently was no difference in the level of expectation and confidence of these people from that of the ones who were healed. Yet, for some reason, they did not regain their health. It is appropriate to mention parenthetically that these "healers" do not claim to possess healing power, but they say that God has given them a gift and it is his power that comes through them. In other words, they do not heal, God heals. It is true, too, that no one of them promises or guarantees healing; they all acknowledge that for some mysterious reason some are healed and some are not.

The experiment Dr. Grad conducted with the persons who were in a depressed psychological state indicated that one's mood or attitude may be a factor in spiritual healing. The religious teachings coming from Jesus about relationship between faith and healing may be significant here. A positive attitude toward healing, which is an aspect of faith, may facilitate the healing process. A belief that healing is not possible, that is, a lack of faith, may depress the healing process. Yet everyone who has had even superficial contact with the healing phenomenon realizes that a simple equation cannot be drawn between faith and healing. Some people with much faith and confidence in the possibility of spiritual healing are not healed, whereas some who have little faith and confidence are healed. There is no simple solution to this question; in fact, it appears to me that at this time the question cannot be resolved.

My personal opinion about the healing phenomenon and the ministry of the church is that a healing ministry is a legitimate part of the total Christian ministry. Prayers for the specific needs of persons who are ill should be made in the context of other congregational prayers in worship. The ritual practice of the laying on of hands also seems appropriate. But the church should make several things very clear as it conducts this ministry. There is no way that spiritual healing can be guaranteed. There is no simple relationship between faith and healing. One who is healed through spiritual means cannot be judged to have greater faith than one who is not. And spiritual healings should be sought as a complement to medical healing. No one interested in spiritual healing should counsel or encourage one who is ill to neglect or to cease medical treatments and to rely solely on spiritual means of healing.

It appears to me that there are various ways by which persons can be healed from illness. Certainly the medical profession has demonstrated its competence in helping people to recover from illness. There is evidence that the ministries of certain "gifted" healers have helped people to regain health. There is additional evidence that prayer will help the healing process. And there is strong support for the fact that a person's emotional state will affect the healing process. All these factors may complement one another in healing. If I became ill, I would accept the advice of my doctor, I would request the prayers of the church, I would attend healing services, if possible, and I would attempt to maintain a high level of confidence throughout the course of my illness. I believe that all these factors may facilitate the healing process.

Spiritual ministrations for healing, it seems to me, are not simply means by which a person's mood is elevated, although if it were just this, it would still contribute to the healing process. However, I believe there is sufficient experimental evidence to conclude that some healing force may be mediated through some persons that may encourage the healing process. This mysterious healing force may be the factor which swings the balance from illness to health in certain situations.

5

PERSONAL SURVIVAL

I know that some readers who have been interested in the material in the previous chapters will have trouble with some subjects in this one. For a variety of reasons people find it very difficult to consider mediums, séances, and subjects such as reincarnation from an objective point of view. But if a person is to look at the subject matter of parapsychology, he must at some time give serious consideration to the theory of personal survival after death and the phenomena that suggest this possibility. Furthermore, there is a practical reason for considering this. A friend sent me a newspaper clipping that reported that a young man who had been murdered led his father to the person who had committed the crime. According to the father, the dead youth spoke to him and guided him to the man who eventually was apprehended and charged with murder. When you read such a news article, how do you interpret it? If you seek an explanation for such a phenomenon, you must consider the possibility of psychic events that involve discarnate personalities. Then, too, occasionally what is represented as communication with the dead through a medium breaks into the news. The supposed communication of Bishop Pike with his deceased son is an example of this. How do you evaluate such a report when you receive it? You have no basis for evaluating it objectively unless you are willing to look seriously at such a phenomenon. The major questions, then, in this chapter are these: Does the human personality survive death? and, Is communication possible between those who survive death and those who still live as human beings?

When a person's brain ceases to function at death, consciousness lapses. The empirical evidence seems to indicate that at that time life terminates. The logical, reasonable conclusion is that after the body and the brain die, nothing remains alive. But in the face of this materialistic conclusion, many persons of differing persuasions have made a faith affirmation—man survives death. Is this affirmation reasonable, or is it simply a product of man's desire for immortality? What evidence is there from psychic experience that may lend credence to the faith affirmation that man survives death?

MEDIUMISTIC COMMUNICATIONS

Trance mediumship is an unusual phenomenon; very few people possess the ability to practice it. Furthermore, it is a phenomenon that is suspect because many persons who claim to be adept at it have been exposed as fraudulent. Yet a few have exhibited abilities that seem to be authentic. Arthur Ford, whose name was publicized as one of the persons Bishop Pike used to contact his son, was such a medium.

Arthur Ford reports that he discovered his psychic abilities during World War I when he was a young army officer. He began to visualize on waking from sleep in the morning the list of men who had died the previous night from influenza. Invariably the envisioned list matched the real roster Lieut. Ford picked up from the adjutant's office.[1] At first he was puzzled by these experiences, but eventually he understood and developed his gift. Through the years until his recent death he had displayed unusual ability as a trance medium.

What happens at a séance with a trance medium? The medium seems to be talking in his sleep. What apparently has happened is that he has placed himself in a hypnotic trance. A discarnate personality supposedly speaks through the medium, bringing messages from other persons who have died to the "sitters" seated with the medium.[2] In a séance, then, communication purports to involve at least four people, two discarnate personalities and two carnate persons. On the "other side" are the discarnate originator of the message and the discarnate control who speaks through the medium. From this side of death are the medium and the sitter. When Arthur Ford, the medium, went into trance, a discarnate personality named Fletcher, who was his control, by some means used the medium's vocal cords to convey messages from discarnate personalities to the sitters.

In October, 1968, my wife and I had a sitting with Arthur Ford in his Philadelphia apartment. A number of persons communicated with us. The conversation was recorded on tape, and an accurate record was transcribed from the tape.

The sitting that we had began with the pleasantries one expects when people meet for the first time. We said, "Hello," and Fletcher, the control, responded. Then, through the medium, Fletcher began to tell us some things about ourselves. He mentioned that someone where he was said she was the one after whom Trudy had been named. This could have been her aunt or grandmother. He correctly identified a spot where scar tissue had formed from a minor surgical procedure. And he gave me some advice about my ministry. Then he told about an older man who had had a brief contact with me in college. He described the nature of this contact, and he correctly identified the place of this man's death. He was incorrect when he said this man knew my father. He said next that my grandfather was there and correctly identified him as a member of a Pennsylvania Dutch plain sect. He spoke about the sale of some land in which our family would be involved. He said the land would be sold, which turned out to be accurate, but said, too, that a portion of the land would be retained, which was inaccurate. Then he said that one of us had a brother who had died in infancy. This was incorrect. He talked about my mother-in-law and identified her final illness, but he said she was in a coma before her death and this was not true. Then he spoke of a good friend of hers who had preceded her in death. After this he said to Trudy: "I guess your father is still living, isn't he?" Trudy told him that her father had died a year before, but there was no further mention of her father.

The control then began to talk about a friend who had died a short time before the sitting. He mentioned the nationality of her name but not the name itself, and said a few things about the circumstances of her death. At this point we responded with too much information, but later, without our prompting, he did supply some other details about her that were correct. Then he talked about the wife of an acquaintance who had died accidentally.

He correctly identified my contact with this man, and he accurately gave a detailed account of the accident. He was incorrect when he said I had met the wife.

The control then began to talk about a doctor from the era of the Revolutionary War who was supposedly an ancestor of Trudy's and through whom Trudy was related to a minister in Philadelphia. This is the one piece of evidence in the sitting we have been unable to research. We know that the minister is a descendant of this man, but we have not been able to establish a relationship from this doctor to Trudy. The sitting closed with some comments about the future of the church and my future in the church.

In our sitting, there were seven discarnate personalities who communicated with us. Four were relatives, although one of these would have to be termed an ancestor, since the relationship, if it does exist, spans five or six generations. One was a friend who had died just a year before the sitting. The other two were persons who at one time in my life had had a contact with me. My wife and I were able to investigate all the information given in the sitting with the exception of one very important piece of evidence. This was the statement that Trudy is related to a minister in Philadelphia through a doctor who lived at the time of the Revolutionary War. With the exception of this information, everything else in the sitting has been carefully checked. Of the wealth of detailed information given, only five very minor points proved not to be true—he said the man who had a contact with me in college knew my father, and this proved to be false; he said I had met the woman who was killed accidentally, and I had not; he said a part of some property to be sold would be retained by the seller, and it was not; he said my wife or I had a brother who had died as an infant, and this is not true; and he said my mother-in-law was in a coma before she died, and she was not. Everything else said to us in the sitting proved to be accurate.

But, in evaluating the material given in a sitting with a trance medium and offering it as evidence for the personal survival of death, one must go beyond the question of whether or not the information is true. Could this information have been secured in ways other than through communication with discarnate spirits? There are six theories that may explain this phenomenon, and they will be considered in order: conscious fraud—investigation, conscious fraud—guesswork, subconscious thought, extrasensory perception, cosmic consciousness, and genuine communication with discarnate spirits.

1. Fraud—Investigation

This theory is simply that the medium investigates the background of the sitters, and in a feigned trance, that is, in a conscious state, the supposed medium reports the results of his investigations. Arthur Ford knew for approximately six weeks that we would be coming for a sitting. Did he in that time gather facts that he then used in the sitting?

We must admit that all the evidence we have verified could have been obtained through investigation. But could the necessary investigative work be done? If Arthur Ford had contacted a person who knew us and our families quite intimately, he could have obtained much of the information, but such a person probably would have spoken to us about the contact. With no single contact, Mr. Ford would have had to conduct investigations in Philadelphia, Lancaster, and Harrisburg, Pennsylvania. Certain facts would have been very difficult to discover, as we learned when we tried to follow leads to the sources of information. He correctly identified the place of death of one person in a small Pennsylvania town when the obituary for this man and his ecclesiastical record, both of which I saw, listed a larger nearby city as the place of death. Only because I knew the locale was I able to verify where the nursing home was in which he died. Mr. Ford also identified a friend of my mother-in-law, who was remembered by only one member of my wife's family. On another occasion I contacted a person for verification concerning facts about his family, and he suggested that since all the information Mr. Ford gave was in the newspaper reports of a tragic event, the medium had simply secured his information from this source and recited it in our sitting. However, it is worth noting that Mr. Ford not only gave correct information concerning names and events that were in the newspaper, but also correctly identified my contact with this man in an organization in which our memberships overlapped for about a year some seven years prior to the sitting. This fact would have been rather difficult to research.

In addition, if Arthur Ford had conducted an investigation into our past, he would certainly have learned that neither of us had brothers and that Trudy's father was deceased, facts he seemed not to know. In fact, if he had simply been reciting facts discovered by investigation, it is difficult to imagine why he would not use any information about Trudy's father, who had died only eighteen months before the sitting. He could easily have obtained information from many sources about him, and this information would have been very satisfying to Trudy. Yet no such information was offered.

Although the theory of fraud through investigation cannot be completely ruled out, there is substantial evidence that suggests that it is an improbable explanation for at least some of the information offered in this sitting.

2. Fraud—Guesswork

This theory is that the medium simulates a trance, and then by educated guesses and ambiguous statements leads the sitter into a conversation in which the sitter offers much of the significant information. There was one point in the transcript of this sitting where we did provide the significant information. In this sequence Mr. Ford suggested the nationality of the person's name and some things about the circumstances of her death. Without thinking, we gave him the name, her relationship to us, as well as a full description of the incident that caused her death and events that followed her death.

However, in most of the other parts of the transcript, information was given in an unambiguous way, and we did not contribute significant information. This theory, then, can hardly be used to explain the entire sitting.

3. Subconscious Thought

This theory is that the medium's trance is genuine, but that in this trance he recites information from his own subconscious mind, as does a hypnotized subject, and not information from the mind of a discarnate spirit. There are several places where this theory possibly may be applied in the record of this sitting. Arthur Ford in the sitting made some comments about the church and the ministry, and he admitted that these comments coincided with his own ideas about the future of the church. Was this information simply offered from Arthur

Ford's subconscious mind or did his ideas come through his relationship with his control, Fletcher? Either is a possibility.

Another point where this theory may apply is in the reference to the death of Trudy's mother. Arthur Ford subconsciously may have assumed that because she had cancer she was in a coma, drug induced or natural, before she died. However, the actual cause of death was not cancer, and she was not in a comatose state when she died.

In addition, this theory may apply to the section mentioned before concerning the doctor from Revolutionary times who is supposedly my wife's ancestor. This doctor's name was Dr. Harvey. Just before Dr. Harvey was introduced, Arthur Ford asked Trudy her father's name. She responded first by giving his common name, Harvey, then his first and second names, Alfred Harvey. Then after a second query from the medium, she gave his full name, Alfred Harvey Simmons. We learned later that the information linking Dr. Harvey to a minister in Philadelphia had been given in a sitting some years before. It is possible that subconsciously my father-in-law's name, Harvey, was associated with information about Dr. Harvey from the Revolutionary War era that had been given in a previous sitting. If there proves to be no genealogical link between Trudy and Dr. Harvey, this would be the most logical explanation for this information. However, this theory could not be used to explain most of the information given in the sitting. Arthur Ford could not have had all the information about our families stored in his subconscious mind unless he had previously conducted an extensive investigation.

Some psychic investigators say that even in the best sittings the medium's subconscious mind runs along with the conversation and at points interjects information. This may account for some of the inaccurate or trivial information given in sittings.[3] But it cannot possibly account for all the information that came in this sitting.

4. Extrasensory Perception

This theory is that the medium in trance can, through extrasensory perception, gather information from the conscious and subconscious parts of the sitters' minds. This information, then, is given back in the sitting. The ESP theory has been confirmed in some investigations. S. G. Soal tells of a series of sittings with a particular medium that he entered with certain fragmentary information about a person. The medium confirmed this information, and the story became more definite and more detailed in his mind. The story developed through several sittings until independent investigation proved that the account was completely false. Then in a subsequent sitting no further information on this was given. It is apparent that in those sittings there was an unconscious telepathic fabrication between the medium's and the sitter's minds. Soal's conclusion as a psychic investigator is that in 90 percent of the cases mediums "read" the sitters' minds, and only rarely do they tell them anything that is not in their conscious or subconscious memories.[4]

Can this theory account for the information given in our sitting? Or, were facts given that were unknown to the sitters? There were several facts that were not in the memories of the sitters: the place of death for the man who knew me in college, the details of a fatal accident that took the life of an acquaintance's wife, and all the information about Dr. Harvey.

I learned, too, from friends who had had sittings with

Arthur Ford that through the medium they received communications from persons they did not know had died. Extrasensory perception could hardly account for this, for they thought these persons were still alive. Bishop Pike in his sitting with Arthur Ford had the same experience.[5] It is significant, too, that in Bishop Pike's second sitting with Arthur Ford details concerning his son's death were given and later verified that could not have come to the medium through a telepathic link with the sitters' minds.[6] This ESP theory may account for some of the information given in a good sitting, but it cannot account for all of it.

A corollary to the ESP theory is that the medium "reads" not only the sitters' minds but the minds of other persons as well. Of course, it is possible that in a sitting Arthur Ford could reach out telepathically to other minds. Certainly, all the information given in a sitting is stored in someone's mind somewhere. The problem with this corollary is a practical one. How would the sitter choose which mind to contact and what information to extract from that person's memory?

The extrasensory perception theory, then, may apply to some information given in a sitting, but this theory seems inadequate to explain the entire phenomenon.

5. Cosmic Consciousness

Some persons have suggested a theory that every event leaves some kind of psychic tracing on a cosmic mind or consciousness. The medium in a sitting, according to this theory, is able to pick out relevant information from this cosmic mind to report to the sitters. There are no surviving personalities on the "other side," this theory says; there is only a cosmic consciousness.

This formulation can hardly be proved or disproved. Certainly such a theory could account for everything communicated in a sitting. The problem with the theory is that it is more difficult to conceptualize than the theory that the communication is genuine. How, for example, can the medium sift through the information accumulated in a cosmic consciousness to pick out what is relevant for a certain sitter? And is it not more difficult to conceptualize such a cosmic consciousness than it is to believe that what happens in a sitting is authentic communication between the spirit of a person who has survived death and the sitter? This theory cannot be ruled out as impossible, but it is an improbable theory.

6. Communication with Surviving Personalities

The one theory remaining is that in a sitting one communicates with personalities who have survived death. It has been shown that each of the other theories is inadequate as an explanation for what happened in our sitting with Arthur Ford. But could a combination of two or more theories account for all the information? It is improbable that as many as four theories, the first four, would all be operating in a sitting. But even if they were, there is one bit of verified information that could not be accounted for, that is, the place of death mentioned previously for one who communicated with us. However, proof of survival after death cannot be built on this one fact, for Arthur Ford may have secured this information from a person in a previous sitting.

The unverified information linking Trudy to Dr. Harvey, if and when it is verified, would be substantial evidence for survival. This information could hardly have been secured in any other way than communication with discarnate personalities. But one cannot build a conclusion on this information until the facts are verified.

The conclusion I have reached after carefully investigating this sitting is that it does offer significant evidence that supports the theory of survival after death. I cannot believe that Arthur Ford deliberately deceived us. The necessary investigations would have been very difficult to make. Furthermore, what motive would he have for doing this? His reputation was well established, and we gave him no money for our sitting. It seems to me that three forces could possibly have been active in the sitting. Some of the information may have come from the medium's subconscious mind; some of it may have come through ESP from the sitters' memories; but some of it, I believe, came from discarnate personalities through the control named Fletcher. These personalities have survived death. I realize that my conclusion cannot be offered as proof of survival, but I believe there is sufficient evidence here to point toward that conclusion.

What kind of evidence from a medium would prove survival? Some suggest that the phenomenon known as cross correspondence is proof. This is described with an example by S. Ralph Harlow in his book *A Life After Death*. The discarnate spirit was a man named Walter Stinson. The medium was Walter's sister, Margery Crandon.

In this spectacular phenomenon (cross correspondence), . . . a so-called "spirit" communicates simultaneously with several mediums separated by long distances, sometimes hundreds of miles. He chops his message into as many parts as there are receivers or mediums, and sends one part to each of them. When the portions are joined they make the complete message. In essence this is thought transference, but instead of being between humans it is between a spirit and several humans.

The particular case of cross correspondence that I witnessed involved three groups—those of us with Margery in Boston; a group 400 miles away in Niagara Falls, New York, with the medium Dr. Henry Hardwicke; and a group 175 miles away in New York City with George Valentine, a man of remarkable psychic powers. . . .

We saw Margery go into trance about 9:30 and Walter chatted with us for a few minutes, greeting those who were in the circle and commenting, "Well, I'm going to have to move like lightning tonight. I've got to watch over you people here even while I go to Niagara Falls and New York. Now here's what I'm going to do. I'll give Margery an arithmetic problem and part of a sentence. The answer to the problem and the words necessary for the completion of the sentence will be deposited in New York and Niagara Falls. You have your arrangements made for getting the other parts back here to you."

We nodded in the séance room, and almost immediately—at 9:52 P.M., according to the official transcript of the sitting—Margery picked up a pencil and wrote, "11 x 2". Beneath it she wrote "kick a dead"—then stopped writing. That was all, and Walter was no longer with us at 10 Lime Street. All members of the group signed this sheet to validate the experiment and Dr. Crandon telephoned the Valentine group in New York City.

There Dr. T. H. Pearson . . . reported that at exactly 9:50 Valentine had written, "equals 2," and "no one ever stops to." The message was signed, "Walter."

Not much later a telegram from the Hardwicke group in Niagara Falls reported to us. At precisely 9:50 Dr.

Hardwicke had gone into trance. With his right hand still in contact with the left hand of his neighbor, he picked up a pencil and wrote rapidly and accurately on two sheets of paper in the center of the table. One sheet read, "2." On the other was the word "horse."

We assembled the three parts. It was not difficult, for not a word was missing or confused. The arithmetic problem read, "11 x 2 equals 22." The sentence, which Margery later told us was one of Walter's favorite sayings when he was alive, was, "no one ever stops to kick a dead horse." [7]

Some critics, however, point out that, remarkable as cross correspondence is, it cannot be used as proof of survival. Dr. Harlow ventures the opinion that cross correspondence involves thought transference between a spirit and several humans. However, it is possible that a person in trance could, through thought transference, convey the parts of a message to others in trance without the aid of a discarnate personality. Cross correspondence, then, constitutes additional evidence for survival but not proof that man survives death.

Is there any evidence from mediumistic communications that would verify the fact of survival after death? Gardner Murphy, in *Three Papers on the Survival Problem*, says that the most cogent type of survival evidence is that which takes the form of postmortem interaction of two or more communicators. He writes:

Some years ago I tried to contrive a plan for survival evidence based on this principle: let us say that Paul Kempton, of Tulsa, Oklahoma, Pierre Leclerc, of Pawtucket, Rhode Island, Angus MacGregor, of Sterling, Scotland, and Leslie Durand, of the Isle of Wright, meet on the "other side." They wish to give evidence to their families. Checking over their various life activities they discover they all had one thing in common: they all had made collections of rare old Wedgwood china. No living human being ever knew they had this *in common;* it is the kind of fact that could be ascertained post-mortem, but not before. It is true that the method would be laborious, and that the practical difficulties of carrying out the plan would be great; indeed, an attempt to give just such a test through Mrs. Leonard did not meet with a notable success. But if such a plan did succeed it would be worth almost any amount of labor.[8]

There is one communication called the "Ear of Dionysius" case reported by Dr. Murphy that does seem to involve cooperation between discarnate personalities.[9] This communication reported in the *Proceedings* of the Society for Psychical Research, Vol. XXIX, came through the mediumship of Mrs. Willett. It involves a story that developed from elements of classical literature and was communicated in sittings over a period of more than a year. The postmortem cooperation was between A. W. Verrall and Professor Henry Butcher. The whole story is filled with classical elements very familiar to Mr. Verrall, but interwoven with these items there appeared appropriate references to Aristotle's *Poetics,* and to other Aristotelian associations characteristic of Professor Butcher. All the facts given were unknown to Mrs. Willett. Even Mrs. Verrall and the other scholars studying the scripts failed to understand the allusions until the final clue was given. This constitutes very strong evidence for survival.

Mediumistic communications provide substantial evidence for personal survival after death. So far, however, nothing can be reported from this source that would constitute proof strong enough to convince a determined skeptic. But there is good evidence that makes the theory that in some form the personality of a man does survive death credible to those who are willing to consider the phenomenon with an open mind.

But how open-minded should a person be? Anyone who publicizes the fact that he has visited a medium will sooner or later meet a person who reminds him about the Biblical admonitions not to visit mediums and wizards. When I first confronted this attitude, I was ready to discount it, but the more experiences I have in this field, the more I realize there is some wisdom in this admonition. I do not accept the reasoning of some people who class all of parapsychology as the "work of the devil." Nor can I accept the careful distinction some people make between legitimate practices—spiritual healing, prayer, ESP experiments—and evil practices—telling the future (precognition) and visiting mediums. But there are possible dangers in consulting mediums. One peril is that not everything the medium says is true. Of course, many persons who claim to be mediums are fraudulent, and their word cannot be trusted. Even those who are not fraudulent are not infallible. A person may approach a sitting with the feeling that since the communication is coming from those who are freed from the limitations of an earthly perspective, what they say will be completely accurate. This is not true, and anyone who does not attempt to verify everything before accepting it is exposing himself unnecessarily to danger. Another peril in visiting mediums exists for people who have recently had a close relative die. Through the medium the bereaved tries to maintain a contact with his deceased relative. This may prevent him from working through his grief and so moving beyond his loss to live a productive life.

The reason that Biblical writers warned the people not to visit mediums was that what they said could not be trusted. I believe that one should heed this warning and not accept uncritically what a medium reports from the "other side." I do, however, think that some things that are said in sittings lend some support to the belief that man survives death, and it is this evidence which warrants the serious investigation of this phenomenon.

In addition, because some people "play" with instruments that are supposed to provide a means of communication with spirits, I feel compelled to say a word about ouija boards and such objects. From my limited experience with ouija boards, I have concluded that for the most part they work through autosuggestion. In other words, I believe that in most cases our subconscious minds make the planchette move across the board. Buried in everyone's subconscious mind are thoughts and feelings he finds unacceptable. Sometimes in ouija sessions these thoughts and feelings have come out. A sufficient number of people have got into serious psychological difficulty through the use of a ouija board to warn us that these instruments may not be "innocent toys." Most serious students of parapsychology strongly advise people not to use ouija boards and such instruments. Some believe, as I do, that the danger is psychological. Others believe "mischievous spirits" influence the results and purposely mislead people, taking them into difficult situations. Whichever is true, it is not a good practice to "play" with such "toys."

APPARITIONS

To understand what constitutes an apparition, you must make an epistemological distinction that you do not usually make when you perceive objects in the physical world. In perception there are two elements—a material object and the sense-data related to it. Normally we do not distinguish between the two. Only in the case of an illusion, when a person draws a false conclusion from sense-data, do we recognize the role the perceiver plays in constructing an image in the act of perception. People interpret the sense-data that come to them and from these form a mental image of a material object; usually they interpret the data correctly, and the image is a reasonable facsimile of the object, but sometimes they interpret these incorrectly. In every case people do not have a direct acquaintance with the physical object itself but only with an image of it formed from their own sense-data.[10] I may look out of the window and see my neighbor walking across his yard. There is a man there, the physical object that originates the perception. But it is possible under certain conditions—perhaps my view is obstructed, or my glance is hurried—that this man is not my neighbor. In my mind I make certain assumptions, and those assumptions, coupled with the sense-data I receive, produce a mental image that may or may not be accurate. So, in normal perception there is a physical object, and there is a group, or groups, of sense-data that are private to the observer and are interpreted by him.

What occurs in the case of an apparition is that all the sense-data for a material thing are present, but there is no physical object. Since no physical object occupies the space where one "sees" an apparition, there can be no reflected light waves or physical sound waves to convey the sense-data to the perceiver.[11]

Yet even though an apparition lacks physical properties,

sense-data similar to those in normal perception arise. G. N. M. Tyrrell, in his classic study of apparitions, in which he uses the information found in the Census of Hallucinations collected by the Society for Psychical Research, has constructed a picture of the perfect apparition from the evidence reported by those who have observed such figures. He notes the points of resemblance between the "Perfect Apparition" and a normal human being if they were standing side by side.

(1) Both figures would stand out in space and would appear equally real and solid. . . .

(2) We would be able to walk around the apparition, viewing it from any distance and from any standpoint. . . .

(3) If the light happened to be poor, both figures would be badly seen, and if more light were turned on, both figures would appear brighter. . . .

(4) Both figures would obscure the background.

(5) If the apparition happened to be wearing a rose in its buttonhole, we would probably smell the scent of it. . . .

(6) On approaching the apparition, we should hear it breathing, and we should hear the rustle of its clothes as it moved and its shoes would shuffle on the floor. . . .

(7) The apparition would probably behave as if aware of our presence. . . .

(8) The apparition might speak to us. . . .

(9) If a mirror were fixed on the wall, we should see the apparition reflected in it. . . .

(10) Both figures would probably cast shadows, but the evidence on this point is uncertain.

(11) If we were to shut our eyes or turn away our head, the apparition would disappear just as the figure by its side would do. And on reopening them, we should see it again.

(12) In addition to its clothes, the figure might have other accessories. . . .

(13) The apparition might pick up any object in the room or open and close the door. We should both see and hear these objects moved; yet physically they would never have moved at all.

(14) For one thing, as soon as we came near the apparition, or if the apparition touched us, we might feel a sensation of cold.

(15) If we tried to take hold of the apparition, our hand would go through it without encountering any resistance. . . .

(16) If we were to sprinkle French chalk on the floor and could induce the apparition and the human being to walk on it together, we should find that only the real man left any footprints, although we should hear the footsteps of both.

(17) If we were to take a photograph of the two figures, only the real man would come out. And if we had sound recording apparatus, only the sounds made by the real man would be recorded. . . .

(18) After a time, which might be anything up to half an hour or so, the apparition would disappear. . . .

(19) Sometimes we should probably find that the apparition did not imitate the behaviour of the material man quite so closely. It might, for instance, become slightly luminous; it might show small details of itself when we were so far away from it that normally we could not possibly have seen them; it might even so far forget itself as to make us see it through the back of our heads.[12]

This collected evidence suggests that an apparition is a psychological phenomenon. It is similar to a material figure, and may be mistaken for one, but it appears not to be material in character.

In his book, Tyrrell identifies four classes of apparitions: experimental cases in which a person deliberately tries to make his apparition visible to a particular percipient, cases in which someone sees the apparition of a person who is undergoing some crisis, cases in which someone sees an apparition of a person who has died a sufficient length of time previously so the apparition cannot be associated with the crisis of death, and apparitions that seem habitually to haunt certain places.[13] Apparitions that occur spontaneously usually fall into the second category, and the crisis that precipitates them frequently is death.

Apparitions seem to cluster around the moment of death These crisis apparitions may be divided into two classes: apparitions of persons undergoing a crisis which are seen by a relative or friend, and apparitions of relatives or friends, sometimes deceased, which appear to a person at the time of death. Tyrrell, as well as other writers, presents cases of the first type, but in his book he does not treat the second of these in any detail. But the Parapsychology Foundation, Inc., under the direction of Karlis Osis, has made a study of deathbed apparitions, which is drawn from the observations made by doctors and nurses of this phenomenon.

Some interesting facts develop from the study of deathbed apparitions that have a bearing on a survival hypothesis. The first is that this phenomenon occurs usually when the physiological and psychological equilibrium of the patient is not markedly disturbed.[14] The visions, then, seem not to be caused by sedation, medication, delirium, or impaired consciousness.

Another significant observation is that a belief in life after death seems to be a factor in this phenomenon. This could mean either that religious people who believe in life after death expect visions, and their expectation produces them, or that their practice of religion has produced a sensitivity toward a transcendent reality that emerges in visions.[15] It would seem that the apparition is to some degree controlled by the beliefs of the observer, for it conforms to what he expects in the future life; at least the vision does not contradict the convictions a person has about life after death.

Of special interest for the survival hypothesis in the study of deathbed apparitions is what is called "Peak in Darien" cases. It sometimes happens that a person who is dying "sees" a relative or a friend who has died but whose death is unknown to the patient. This phenomenon has been used as a proof of survival, for the person dying would have no way of knowing that the friend or the relative had died except by "seeing" the spirit that had survived death. This supposition has been strengthened by the conviction many psychic investigators have held that only the dead are seen in deathbed apparitions.[16] However, the Osis study reveals that living persons as well as deceased personalities appear in such visions, and this cuts the ground from under the use of "Peak in Darien" cases as evidence for survival.[17] Such cases are not without significance for the survival hypothesis, but the case for survival will not stand on these alone.

Before we consider further the significance of apparitions for the survival hypothesis, it is necessary to review the theories for apparitions. The theory that the apparition is a material entity must be rejected, since these figures do not have all the properties of ordinary material objects; for example, they cannot be touched or held. So the explanation for apparitions should be psychological in nature. F. W. H. Myers in 1888 put forth the theory that apparitions are telepathic phenomena. He theorized that a person undergoing a crisis might send a telepathic message to a percipient who visualized the message in sensory form.[18]

The chief difficulty with this theory is that a fair number of apparitional cases are perceived at the same time by two or more persons, and it seems improbable, under this theory, that more than one person would see the same apparition at the same time and place.

To account for this difficulty, Myers added a corollary to his theory. He said that apparitions, though not material, have a psychical element that occupies space and can be perceived by an unknown form of supernormal perception, not necessarily through sense organs. Myers' theory, then, is a hybrid—partly psychological and partly psychical. And the psychical element comes close to being a physical form. Edmund Gurney rejected the psychical or physical element of Myers' theory and tried to improve upon his formulation by saying that in collective perceptions the agent telepathically influences the primary percipient, who, though creating his own sensory image, acts as an agent by transmitting the apparition on to a secondary percipient, who then retransmits the apparition on to another, and so on. Gurney describes the process as an apparition spreading by "infection." The objection to this theory was raised by Myers, namely, that there is no independent evidence that apparitions tend to spread by "infection."

A more complex and more adequate theory has been produced by G. N. M. Tyrrell. The problem he considers is that the agent, even though he can have no detailed idea in his mind of how he appears to another, does indeed appear that way, and in addition he appears in and is aware of the percipient's surrounding, of which he as a rule can know little or nothing. Since the apparition appears sometimes in a context unfamiliar to him, the apparition cannot be merely a direct expression of an agent's idea, but it must be a drama worked out by an agent and a percipient.[19]

According to this theory, the agent at the moment of crisis does not think of the percipient except in general terms. The work of constructing the apparition drama is done by the percipient in a region of the personality below the level of consciousness. Tyrrell explains his theory further by postulating two metaphorical figures in the mental process of the percipient. One he called the "producer," that something in the mind which works out the idea in dramatic form, and the other an "executor" or "stage-carpenter," the something-else within the mind which expresses this drama in the sensory form of apparition.[20] The apparition, then, is a joint effort between an agent and a percipient. It may include elements known only to the agent, as a wound received by the agent that is unknown to the percipient. Or it may include elements known only to the percipient, as a symbol that relates to the agent's situation but is not part of his physical surroundings. So an apparition may contain a coffin to symbolize death, even though no coffin is in the area where the agent is; such a symbol would have to be produced by the percipient's mind.[21] Tyrrell believes that the correlation between agent and percipients in apparitions seen by two or more people takes place telepathically. He admits the difficulty of picturing the way this takes place. It means that the minds of at least three people work together to produce a mental image that is the same for all three. This theoretical formulation adequately explains most of the characteristics of apparitions, but it does leave the problem of accepting the fact that minds of different persons can cooperate to produce identical mental images.

Another theory for apparitions that is current today is similar to Myers' theory. It says that the apparition is a psychic or quasi-physical entity that may be perceived by normal or supernormal means of perception. This theory suffers from the fact that such a substance is unknown in science. The final verdict on these theories cannot be given until we know more about mental processes and the nature of matter.

The significance of apparitions for the survival hypothesis is open to question. A person who has seen the apparition of a friend who has died may accept this as absolute proof that the friend has survived death. But persons making a careful inquiry cannot leap to that conclusion. Solid evidence for survival given by an apparition must meet the same test as evidence from a medium; that is, does the apparition reveal anything that only a surviving personality could know? Tyrrell reports a number of such cases.

In addition, there are two classic cases of apparitions that have conveyed information unknown to the percipient. These are often cited in the literature on this subject. The one case involves a salesman who in 1876 in his hotel room in St. Joseph, Missouri, saw an apparition of his sister, who had died nine years before. The apparition was very close to him, and he could perceive her features distinctly. He particularly noticed a bright red scratch three-fourths of an inch long on the right side of her nose. When he returned home, this man related to his parents what he had seen, and at the mention of the scratch his mother almost fainted. When she regained her composure, she said that after her daughter's death she accidentally made a scratch on her daughter's body when doing a small act of devotion. She was very much disturbed that she had unintentionally marred the features of her dead daughter, and she carefully obliterated all traces of the scratch with the aid of powder. She never mentioned this to anyone. The scratch that this man observed on the apparition was not something he knew about his sister, and this constituted some evidence for the survival thesis.

The other famous case is known as the Chaffin will case. In 1905, James L. Chaffin, a North Carolina farmer, made a will, attested by witnesses, leaving his farm to one of his four sons, with no provisions made for the other three or for his wife. In 1919, he made a second will, which was not witnessed but was in his handwriting, dividing his property equally among his four children, with the provision that they take care of their mother. Mr. Chaffin placed the will in a Bible that belonged to his father. After he died in 1921, his first will was accepted as legally valid and his property was given to the one son. Four years later, another of Mr. Chaffin's sons began to have vivid dreams in which his father appeared at his bedside but did not speak. Then one time he appeared in a dream and said, "You will find my will in my overcoat pocket." This son looked for the overcoat, and when he found it, he discovered in one pocket a note in his father's handwriting: "Read the 27th chapter of Genesis in my Daddy's old Bible." He had some trouble finding the Bible, but when he finally located it, he discovered the 1919 will in the place indicated. This will was then admitted to probate.[22] In this incident a fact known only to the deceased man was communicated to his son.

These cases and other similar ones provide further evidence for survival after death. But this evidence might not meet the rigid requirements of science. So again it may be more discreet to say that there is evidence here for survival but not proof of it. Nevertheless, as evidence is accumulated from different sources, the survival hypothesis becomes more plausible.

OUT-OF-BODY EXPERIENCES

The phenomenon called out-of-body experiences is sometimes cited as evidence for the survival hypothesis. Spontaneous out-of-body experiences sometimes occur when a person has nearly died and has remembered, after regaining consciousness, experiences he had while in an apparently lifeless condition. A number of such cases have been recorded in the research files of associations for psychic studies and in literature relating to psychic matters.[23] One example comes from *How to Make ESP Work for You*, in which the author, Harold Sherman, reports a personal experience he had in 1920. He had gone to his physician for a lancing operation which was to take place in his office. Mr. Sherman received general anesthesia for this operation. After he lost consciousness, he "awoke" in the air above his body. Beside him was his brother, who had died six years before. He was able to see and hear what was going on around his body—the doctor was greatly concerned and the nurse reported that she felt no pulse. Suddenly, when his brother took his arm, Mr. Sherman realized that he must be dead. He pulled away from his brother, saying, as he did so: "No,

Edward, I can't go with you. Mother and Dad don't know anything about this. I'm not ready. I can't die now." As he thought of his parents, he blacked out. He next perceived himself walking down the main street of the city where his father had a business establishment. The people on the street paid no attention to him. He entered the store, and no one, including his father, noticed him. He put his hand on his father's shoulder and said, "Dad," but he got no response. He thought of his mother. There was another blackout, after which he found himself in his parents' home, where his mother was preparing a meal in the kitchen. He spoke to his mother but got no response. He then decided to return to his physical form. In that instant he had a traveling sensation and regained consciousness in his body, which the doctor and nurse were treating.[24] This experience, if authentic, is very suggestive in forming an opinion of the relationship between the physical (earth) and psychical (heaven) worlds. But are these experiences what they seem to be?

The classic theory to explain out-of-body experiences is that a person has two bodily forms—a physical form and a psychical form, which is sometimes called a spiritual body (I Cor. 15:44) or an astral body. The second, or psychic body, is purportedly an exact duplication of the physical body except for the blemishes. Some people theorize that it is composed of a type of matter in which the electrons move at a higher rate of vibration than those which make up conventional matter. According to this theory, under certain conditions—sleep, trance, coma—the psychic body may detach itself from the physical body and travel around independently.[25] But is this the only explanation which may be given for the out-of-body phenomenon? A possible alternate theory is that these experiences are a result of telepathy plus clairvoyance. So Mr. Sherman, in the detailed experience quoted above, could have perceived telepathically, and therefore subconsciously, what was occurring around him when he was unconscious. He could have viewed the scenes in the doctor's office, his father's store, and his home through clairvoyance.

C. J. Ducasse, in his excellent study on the belief of life after death, says that out-of-body experiences do not prove that a person can exist apart from his physical body. These phenomena do, however, support the more modest but still amazing conclusion that when a person's eyes are closed and he is asleep, he may at times perceive physical events and objects, including his own body, from some point in space around them.[26] But Dr. Ducasse, in making this summation on out-of-body experiences, does not rule out the possibility of the theory of two bodily forms, physical and psychical, to explain this. He merely says it is not the only possible explanation.

Here, again, as has been done before in this chapter, it is necessary to distinguish between proof and evidence. Out-of-body experiences do not prove that a spiritual or psychic personality can exist apart from the body. They do, however, offer evidence that such an existence may be possible. They point in the direction of some kind of incarnational theory for man, that is, that a spiritual human component inhabits a physical body, and that under certain conditions this spiritual component may exist apart from the body. The possibility that this could occur is necessary for any theory of survival after death.

REINCARNATION

Belief in reincarnation has never been strong in the Western world, but it has been part of the belief structure of Eastern religions. In the mid-1950's, however, a book was published in the United States that sparked popular interest in this subject and initiated a controversy over it. The book was written by Morey Bernstein, who records what occurred when he hypnotized Ruth Mills Simmons (pseudonym for Virginia Burns Tighe) and, by a technique called age regression, took her back beyond her present life-span into what seemed to be a previous lifetime. Mrs. Tighe began to describe episodes of a life in which she was Bridey Kathleen Murphy, an Irish girl born in Cork in 1798. She identified the members of her family, told about her schooling, and related the details of her marriage to Brian Joseph McCarthy. She told where they lived when they moved to Belfast, and she described her life there. She lived to the age of sixty-six and was buried in Belfast in 1864. Mrs. Tighe, it should be mentioned, had never been to Ireland and seemed to have no special knowledge of that land.[27]

The search for Bridey Murphy involved the investigation of this information to see if it was correct. No conclusive evidence was uncovered to prove that Virginia Tighe was once Bridey Murphy, but enough evidence was verified concerning the geography of the area and the customs and language of the people to indicate that Mrs. Tighe somehow had stored in her mind some unusually accurate information about life in Belfast in the nineteenth century.

Some critics of Mr. Bernstein's theory that Mrs. Tighe had lived previously as Bridey Murphy attempted to show that her memories of a previous lifetime were really subconsciously preserved memories of her own childhood interwoven with stories about Ireland supposedly told to her by an aunt. Another critical account supposedly uncovered the real Bridey Murphy—a Mrs. Bridey Murphy Corkell, whose house in Chicago was across the street from one of those in which Virginia had lived. However, the investigation of the claims of the critics showed that they were not totally accurate. These claims and counterclaims are reviewed by C. J. Ducasse in his book *The Belief in a Life After Death*.[28] This situation leaves one in an uncertain state unable really to affirm or deny the claim that Mrs. Tighe was, in a former life, Bridey Murphy. Since the critics could not show a definite source for Mrs. Tighe's information about Bridey Murphy, the reincarnation theory remains a plausible explanation.

It must be stated here that the tactic of using age regression to discover information about previous lifetimes is suspect for many hypnotists. They have discovered that a subject under hypnosis has a strong desire to please his hypnotist by supplying information for all his questions. So long as the hypnotist questions the hypnotized subject in areas of his experience, he will give accurate responses, but when the hypnotist moves into areas not a part of his experience, he may spin fanciful tales, drawing on information he has accumulated from stories, conversations, television, or any other source. So the search for information from previous lifetimes through age-regression hypnosis is hardly a reliable method.

More promising evidence for reincarnation comes from the spontaneous cases, usually among children, of conscious memories from a previous lifetime. Dr. Ian Stevenson, alumni professor of psychiatry at the University of Virginia School of Medicine, has included the record of his investigations of twenty such cases along with his conclusions in a book, *Twenty Cases Suggestive of Re-*

incarnation. It is impossible adequately to treat this excellent record in the short space of a few pages in this chapter. However, in reading the book one is impressed by the very careful and cautious way Dr. Stevenson investigates these cases and formulates his conclusions. The cases investigated occurred in India, Ceylon, Brazil, Lebanon, and among the Tlingit Indians of Southeastern Alaska. It is worth noting that these reports come from cultures where there is long-established belief in reincarnation. Dr. Stevenson has, however, investigated some cases suggestive of rebirth in cultures quite alien to the belief in rebirth. In the majority of these cases it was children from two years of age to nine or ten who had the strongest memories of a previous life. After that age their memories began to fade. Careful investigations could be made, since in most cases only a few years had passed between the death of a person and his alleged rebirth as another person. The child with conscious memories of a previous lifetime was taken to the site where that alleged lifetime occurred to test his memory of persons and places.

The evidence for reincarnation in Dr. Stevenson's book does not depend solely on what the children remembered. There are really four types of evidence: (1) conscious memories of the previous lifetime, (2) the recognition and correct identification of persons and places from the previous lifetime, (3) similar behavioral characteristics, and (4) congenital markings. In nineteen of the twenty cases there were specific, well-defined, and accurate recollections from the alleged previous lifetime. In these cases, when the child was taken to his home in the previous life, he accurately identified members of his previous family and neighbors. In several cases there was a similarity in behavioral traits in the two persons who were allegedly the same person in two lifetimes. One boy had an unconscious and intense fear of two men who had murdered him in his allegedly previous lifetime.[29] Another had an aversion to eating curd, which had been an important contributing cause of the illness and death of the person he allegedly was in a previous lifetime.[30] In another case, the allegedly reincarnated person demonstrated at the early age of five a definite skill for sewing, which had been a talent of the previous personality.[31] Another case revealed a similarity in physical characteristics. A man had been lame, and when the personality that allegedly was this man reincarnated walked, he had a similar gait.[32] Evidential congenital markings appeared in several cases. The case involving the similarity in gait contained evidence of congenital markings too. Both persons had identical prominent birthmarks.[33] In another case, a person bore a birthmark the shape of a spear wound at the place on his right flank where the person he allegedly had been in his previous lifetime had received a fatal spear wound.[34] The evidence for reincarnation in these twenty cases is substantial.

Dr. Stevenson is very careful as he draws conclusions from his studies. He considers a number of possible hypotheses. The opportunities for fraud seem very slight; it would have been particularly difficult to stage the emotional recognition scenes Dr. Stevenson witnessed. Cryptomnesia seems to be more plausible than fraud. According to this theory, the child would somehow have received information through a person or other source which he later "remembered" about the alleged previous family. In some of the cases presented, this is a possibility. However, in many of the cases this theory is inadequate because the information given was rich in quantity and minute in detail. In addition, this theory could not adequately explain the immediate and accurate recognition of persons known in the allegedly previous lifetime.[35] Another possible theory is that of genetic "memory." This theory is that a person "remembers" with visual and other imagery what happened to his forefathers just as a baby bird "remembers" how to fly when it is pushed from the nest. This could apply to several cases in which the allegedly reincarnated personality is a direct descendant of the previous personality. But this theory cannot account for many of the twenty cases Dr. Stevenson presents.

The possible alternate theory Dr. Stevenson discusses at length is extrasensory perception and personation. According to this theory, the subject receives by extrasensory perception information about a previous personality. He then integrates this information into his personality so thoroughly that he comes to believe he is that person.[36] With this theory one need not assume any personal contact between the child and some person familiar with the facts of the previous personality. However, there are difficulties with the theory. One is that in some of these cases all the information known to the child did not reside in any one living person's mind. It is difficult to conceive how a person could draw this material from the minds of several different persons and integrate it into one factual account.[37] In addition, it is difficult in some cases to explain how a person becomes the target for information about a deceased person when the families of the two persons have had absolutely no previous knowledge of one another. For these and other reasons Dr. Stevenson rejects this theory as a possibility in all but the weakest cases.

At this point Dr. Stevenson is left with two possible hypotheses, both of which include the survival theory. They are possession and reincarnation. Possession is the "entering" of a discarnate personality into a carnate personality and influencing to some degree that person's thought.[38] Possession of a person by a discarnate surviving personality is a possibility in these cases. However, in some of them the theory of reincarnation seems more adequate. Possession does not adequately explain the common occurrence of an increased revival of memories when the child returned to the location of the life of the previous personality. A revival in memory seems more natural for a person who is returning to a familiar place. Another problem with the possession theory is that some of the children remembered how buildings were arranged or people looked during the previous existence, but did not recognize changes in appearance. Presumably if a possessing discarnate personality is "hanging around" the site of his terrestrial life, he would keep up to date on changes in buildings and people.[39] On the other hand, in one case that Dr. Stevenson investigated, the person who supposedly was reborn as a reincarnated child died three and one half years after that baby was born.[40] This strongly suggests that this phenomenon is not reincarnation, but possession.

How can we interpret this phenomenon? Dr. Stevenson seems to favor the reincarnation theory. My own preference is for possession. In the Bridey Murphy case the discarnate personality, Bridey Murphy, could have entered Mrs. Tighe's thought when she was in hypnotic trance just as the control enters a medium's thought when he is in trance. In the cases Dr. Stevenson investigated, the discarnate personality could have exercised a dominant influence over a child's thought. But the important thing to note is that the two theories that best describe this phenomenon—reincarnation and possession —both support the supposition that man survives physical death.

CONCLUSION

The matter of survival after death is not, from the scientific point of view, proved. There is substantial evidence that tends to confirm this hypothesis, but that evidence is not sufficiently conclusive to be considered proof. One is tempted to follow the logic of the adage, "Where there is smoke, there is fire." There is plenty of "smoke" apparent to the critical observer who investigates the question of survival, but to say that the "smoke" proves there is a "fire" involves a leap of faith that makes the conclusion unscientific. Nevertheless, that leap of faith is not a leap into the incredible, and it seems to me that it is not an unreasonable conclusion to reach. Belief in life after death seems credible from the evidence presented.

This conclusion means that man is not simply a physical being. The personality resides in a material form. But the personality is not simply a product of that material form, so when the material form dies, the person does not cease to exist. A person's body may be viewed as an instrument that the person uses, just as a musician uses a musical instrument. And as a musician cannot produce music from an instrument that is broken, a personality cannot utilize an organism destroyed by injury or illness. The person or spirit, or whatever the essential being of a man is called, resides in bodily form until that body can no longer be utilized. Then by some means the person is released to another kind of existence.

But the matter of survival is not just a "yes/no" question. If you believe that a person does survive death, many questions remain to be answered.

Where does the spirit come from? Reincarnation provides one answer to that question: the spirit that originated in some form of spiritual creation is successively reborn in bodily form in different eras. If, like me, you reject the concept of preexistence and still believe in survival, you must visualize the creation of a person who is a physio-spiritual being in which the two, body and spirit, are united but not tied so firmly that the activity of the spirit depends on the life of the body.

Another important question related to survival is, What survives death? It is apparent that the body does not. If the spirit survives, what psychological functions survive with it? For example, the capacity to remember past experiences may survive, whereas the capacity for intellectual initiative, critical judgment, and inventiveness may not. There are other possible variations too. There is still not enough known about survival to come to a definite conclusion.

This leads into another question: What is the quality of life after death? The traditional dogma of Christianity has imposed a two- (heaven and hell) or three- (heaven, purgatory, and hell) tiered structure on the afterlife. The quality of life in heaven is viewed as perfection. Psychic investigators raise the possibility that although the quality of life after death may vary from person to person, the various qualities of life are not spatially defined. They generally believe that a person does not change radically after death. He may grow or expand his understanding, but he does not become a radically different person. The selfish do not become unselfish. The angry do not become meek. So life after death is similar to life before death.

One can develop a new quality of life by growing in his ability to love, but this comes slowly through learning opportunities and not suddenly through a radical transformation. The quality of life after death, then, may be determined as is the quality of life before death. "Heaven" and "hell" here are determined by the way a person lives and the company he keeps. It may be that the same is true in the life after death.

Another interesting question related to survival is, How long does the person survive? Traditionally Western religion has said eternally. This may be the case. Or it may be that after a time spirits cease to exist. Another possibility is given in reincarnation, in which a spirit goes through a succession of lifetimes.

There is yet another question that arises: Where are the spirits who have survived? The traditional religious idea is that these spirits have gone to some place that is separated from the earth. Some psychic investigators think otherwise. They say that there is not a separate place for the spirits that have survived. This side and the "other side" are not spatially different. The spirits of surviving persons inhabit the same space as do people in a bodily state. The only difference is that they are invisible to normal vision and they are not spatially bound by material bodies.

Another question develops from this: What is the relationship between spirits who have survived and persons on earth? It seems that those who have survived have an awareness of what is happening on earth; it is possible that they may even influence what occurs. There is also the possibility that through a medium or through prayer and meditation, a person on earth may receive communications from persons on the "other side." This in itself is difficult to illustrate, and to go beyond such a general statement would be unwise.

Much of what I have written in this concluding section is speculation built up like a "house of cards." Pull one of the "cards" away, namely, the one that affirms survival after death, and the whole "house" collapses. But there is some good evidence that the survival "card" should remain in place. Other conjectures may in time prove to be wrong, but in my opinion at least some of them will remain valid.

6

PSYCHIC PHENOMENA
AND RELIGION

This final chapter is a summary and not a conclusion. Certainly I am not ready to reach any conclusions in this field, and I do not know many other people who are. There is much speculation in parapsychology, but as yet there are few solid facts. Throughout this book I have tried to remain as objective as possible in presenting the phenomena and then indicating the possible theories that may be constructed to explain them. Here and there I have indicated my preference, but I have tried to keep my beliefs in the background. In this chapter I want to reveal the convictions that I have formed as a result of my study in this field. I am going to list in a descending order of credibility my beliefs concerning psychic phenomena.

1. There are events in human experience that do not fit the categories that present scientific theories recognize as natural.

I believe this to be an indisputable fact: events do occur that cannot be explained by scientific theories now formulated. The one thing a critic of psychic phenomena cannot say is that they do not occur. Some people have had the experience of perceiving events that could not have been communicated to them by sensory means. Some people *have* received accurate information about what will happen in the future. Some people *have* experienced healing that appears to have come through nonmedical means. These things happen, and only an unreasonably biased critic can deny that they do.

The real controversy, it seems to me, is not over the question, Do psychic phenomena occur? The controversy is over how they occur and how we should interpret them.

2. *Extrasensory perception occurs in human experience.*

I accept this as a fact. An experiment in which the thoughts of a person in one room can produce a measurable physical reaction in a person in a room in another building one eighth of a mile away when there is no means of sensory communication between the two persons is adequate demonstration that extrasensory perception occurs.

3. *Prayer is a valuable religious practice.*

In the chapter on prayer I indicated three possible ways to view prayer—reflective thought, extrasensory communication between persons, or extrasensory communication between a person and a spiritual being. I believe there is good evidence to support the opinion that prayer involves extrasensory communication, that is, that prayer is more than mere reflective thought. I personally believe that the extrasensory communication in prayer involves a spiritual being we call God, but I realize that my personal conviction is not based on the evidence alone. The evidence indicates only that extrasensory communication operates in the prayer phenomenon. But whether this communication is man to man, as some would say, or man to God to man, as I believe, prayer is a valuable and effective religious practice.

4. Healing may occur by nonmedical means through the spiritual ministrations of persons who seem to possess some healing ability.

At this point in my order of credibility I slip from what I judge to be an indisputable fact to what I accept as a highly credible conviction. I believe that spiritual healing happens, but I feel that our knowledge about the healing mechanisms of the body and the effect of the mind upon the body (psychosomatic medicine) is not sufficient for us to conclude with absolute certainty that the healing results from a force mediated by a healing agent. The experiments that have been conducted by Dr. Grad, Sister Justa, and others certainly point in this direction, but I do not believe the scientific proof is as yet conclusive. I feel confident, however, that the day will come when the accumulated evidence will be judged as conclusive proof of a healing force.

5. The psychokinesis (PK) phenomenon, that is, the ability of the mind alone with no known physical contact to exercise some control over a physical object, may occur in human experience.

You may be surprised that I have this fairly high on my order of credibility, since I have not dealt extensively with this phenomenon in previous chapters. Probably I would have put this down a notch or two if I had not come across a book by Dr. Louisa E. Rhine entitled *Mind Over Matter.*[1] I received this book just a week before I finished my work on this material, and I could not include the information in Chapter 2. Dr. Louisa Rhine reviews the range of experiments and tests for PK and makes the case for it highly credible. Even though my own meager experiments for PK did not produce positive results, I am convinced that belief in the "mind over matter" phenomenon is highly credible.

6. There is some, as yet unidentified, force (or forces) that operates in psychic phenomena.

This affirmation is most clearly indicated by the healing phenomenon. Experiments that relate to healing have pointed to some kind of force that has an influence on disease. The prayer experiments with plants also point to the existence of some such force. And certainly psychokinesis could not be explained apart from some unidentified force moving from a mind to a material object. Some psychic phenomena and some experiments in parapsychology certainly indicate that a psychic force exists.

The difficulty in discussing this force is that it has not been identified or measured. It apparently cannot be measured on any of the instruments scientists now use to measure the various forms of energy. It seems, too, that this force does not conform to all the known laws governing energy in the universe. For example, this force seems, according to some experimenters, not to diminish in its power as it travels through space. There have been experiments, too, that suggest that this force can go through a Faraday cage, used to shield against electric fields, as well as the lead-impregnated glass used to shield against radioactive emissions.[2] These two shield against much physical energy, and this suggests that a psychic force must be of a different quality from physical energy. In addition, the psychic force seems to be very directional. Perhaps I can best express this in an illustration. If lightning strikes a tree, the sound of thunder will go out in all directions, and everyone in the area covered by those sound waves will hear it. But an extrasensory communication coming from one person at a particular place perhaps is perceived by only one other person miles away. This force, then, does not produce an effect that is perceived generally.

Can this psychic force be called a type of energy? If energy is defined in a very general way (as many scientists define it) as the ability to do work, that is, the ability to effect something, it may be called "energy." If, however, energy is thought of in terms of known physical forces, then this psychic force should not be identified as "energy."

It does seem plausible that some force exists that operates in psychic phenomena. This force may be an unidentified physical force that operates in our universe, or it may be a force of a different quality that may be called spiritual.

7. *Man is a being who is physical and spiritual in nature.*

It is a toss-up whether I put this statement or the next one first. I set this order because one bit of evidence that does not relate directly to survival, the out-of-body experience, seems to indicate that man has a dual nature. Of course, all the phenomena relating to survival point in this direction too. In my opinion, there is credible evidence that implies that man has a spiritual nature, and that under certain conditions this spiritual nature may exist apart from his physical form.

8. *Persons survive death.*

There are some events that suggest that people live after their physical deaths. It seems to me that the survival hypothesis is the best way to explain these mysterious phenomena. I accept it as credible. But I do acknowledge that evidence from these phenomena does not constitute conclusive proof for survival. I would point out, too, that this evidence for survival does not indicate anything about the quality or length of life for the surviving personality.

9. *The precognition phenomenon points toward a sphere of thought and activity that is beyond the physical sphere and that may include some transcendent spiritual being.*

Precognition, as was pointed out in Chapter 3, is the most perplexing of the ESP phenomena. How can someone know the future? I am not going to repeat the entire argument from Chapter 2, but of the three possible explanations, the one that seems most believable to me is that beyond the physical sphere of life there is a sphere that, at least to some degree, is transcendental and spiritual. This sphere may be the habitation of a spiritual being(s).

I realize that there may be other explanations for this phenomenon, so I cannot affirm this with the certainty I have for some of my earlier statements. I do feel, however, that my convictions here are not incredible.

10. *There is the possibility of personal communication which crosses between the spiritual and the physical spheres of life.*

Some people who have had experience with parapsychology suggest that there are several openings for communication between these two spheres of life. They include prayer and meditation, dreams, apparitions, and trances. I personally believe that some communication by these means is possible. But the problem with affirming this as a highly credible conviction is that one has difficulty separating information that might come from within the mind of the percipient (or by ESP from another person's mind to the percipient's mind) from authentic communication from a spiritual sphere. Therefore, I feel that I can believe this, but I can understand, too, why some people have great difficulty accepting it.

11. Reincarnation, a progression of a spirit from one human life to another, does not occur.

In the last chapter I said that I do not accept reincarnation as a possibility. It may be that my religious background and training prevent me from viewing objectively the phenomena that seem to point to this conclusion. I feel that Dr. Stevenson's investigative work has been marked by rigorous standards and careful procedures. He makes a strong case for reincarnation. But I believe that an equally strong case can be made for explaining this class of phenomena as possession. To me this is more credible. Therefore, I am willing to acknowledge that reincarnation is one theory that may explain a particular class of psychic phenomena, but it is not the only theory that explains it. I personally find one of the other explanations more credible.

Parapsychology is a subject that is filled with speculation and controversy. In this book I have attempted to pick my way very carefully through the subject—to present the phenomena and some of the possible explanations for them. In this chapter, I have tried to present a cautious summary of my own views.

As my interest in the field of psychic phenomena has

grown and people have learned about my studies, I have observed some interesting reactions to the subject. I want to present and discuss some of these reactions.

"I won't consider the possibility of psychic phenomena because they don't fit my view of the world."

The intensity with which people hold this view and their reasons for saying this vary. Some people adopt this attitude because they feel that nothing can happen which in any way challenges the present theories and categories of science. This is akin to the rather arrogant belief that everything worth discovering has already been discovered. Who can live in this day of rapidly expanding knowledge with such an attitude? The limits of our knowledge and understanding are continually expanding. I believe we must continually search for more understanding and knowledge about life in our world.

Some other people react this way because they identify psychic phenomena with superstition, fakery, and fraud. Certainly, as I have indicated, there are fraudulent methods in some occult practices. There are some people, too, who, without any intention to deceive, leap to unwarranted conclusions about psychic phenomena. But there are many responsible and respected investigators working in parapsychology. Their work and their theories deserve the same kind of consideration given to the work of researchers in other fields of endeavor.

There are still other people who for religious reasons refuse to consider that psychic phenomena may be valid. Because psychic phenomena have, in my opinion, a unique relationship to religious faith, I want to consider this in connection with other comments that people have made to me.

"Psychic phenomena are the work of the devil."

I must make a distinction here between two types of people who make such statements. There is one group that says that everything falling under the category of psychic phenomena—ESP, parapsychology experiments, mediumship, ouija boards, clairvoyance, telepathy, precognition, fortune-telling, etc.—is evil. There is another group that draws a line between legitimate practices—the scientific and religious practices related to parapsychology—and evil practices—the occult practices related to parapsychology. It is mediumship, fortune-telling, ouija boards, and any methods used to contact the spirits of the dead that are works of the devil, according to this latter group of people.

You should note that this reaction affirms the validity of psychic events. Most of the people who say that they are the work of the devil believe that psychic phenomena do occur. But they go on to say that these events are the instruments the devil uses to entice people into false beliefs and erroneous religious practices. The devil, they say, is the master of deceit, and he issues true information to entice people and make them devotees of the occult. Then when the people are "hooked," he moves in to destroy them.

There are at least two reasons why people take this position: the Bible warns against mediums who consult the dead, and some people who have become involved in occult practices have been harmed by them.

Most of the Biblical admonitions against mediums and necromancy are in the Old Testament. In Leviticus the writer says that anyone who consults a medium will be cut off from God's people, and anyone who is a medium or wizard should be stoned to death. The reason for this harsh warning may be most clear in Isa. 8:19, where the prophet implies that the word which comes from God is dependable, whereas the word which comes through a medium is not. Yet in the best-known story from the Old Testament involving a medium—the account of Saul's contact with the medium at Endor (I Sam. 28:8-19)—the text says that the medium made contact with the spirit of Samuel, who had died, and that what he said to Saul proved to be accurate. Nevertheless, the Biblical writers viewed this as an evil event, because Saul turned from trusting in God's word to consulting a medium—a practice that on so many occasions had proved untrustworthy and misleading.

I think that this Biblical warning should be taken seriously. There are numerous people claiming to have psychic gifts who are fraudulent. Some of them are so clever in their deceit that an experienced psychic investigator has difficulty discovering it. Even in sittings with mediums who are not deceitful, a person cannot accept everything that is said as truth. In the discussion of our sitting with Arthur Ford, I expressed my opinion that at least three factors affected what was said. The mind of the trance medium seemed to follow along the conversation and may have been responsible for some information, the minds of the sitters seemed to contribute some information communicated by ESP to the medium, and the discarnate control seemed to supply some information. It becomes very difficult to sort out what comes from which source and what information can be trusted. I can see no harm that was done in our sitting with Arthur Ford. Our purpose was to see if any information we received could have come only from the "other side." We tested this information very carefully. However, if a message came to me through a medium giving me advice concerning the future—"Take a new job," "Sell your house," etc.—I would be very careful about following that advice. Mediumship is an interesting phenomenon, but I do not believe the information given through a medium is completely trustworthy.

A second reason for the conviction some people express that psychic phenomena are the work of the devil is that people have been harmed by some of these practices. Hugh Lynn Cayce, in his book *Venture Inward*, recounts several case studies in which people have got into serious difficulty with ouija boards, automatic writing, and such practices.[3] In one case a lady who had been using a ouija board began to hear a voice that said she was in "his" power. "He" threatened to kill her. She became ill because of this experience, and there were sexual overtones to her experience. I have read of another case in which a man claimed that an evil "spirit" attempted to kill him. Other people have told of experiences in which threatening messages came to them, such as that of a young man who received a message from a ouija board that he would kill his fiancée. Some people have reported strange physical phenomena occurring in connection with using a ouija board or practicing automatic writing.

There are two possible explanations for these frightening phenomena, one psychological and one parapsychological. The psychological explanation is that the messages that come are from the suppressive negative thoughts and feelings of hate, fear, and sexual repression that lie buried in a person's subconscious mind. These subconscious repressed thoughts are expressed in the ouija message as the subconscious mind affects the fingers controlling the planchette; these subconscious thoughts sometimes build into frightening psychological phenomena. So the woman who heard the frightening voice was simply hearing from her own mind the thoughts and drives she had repressed. The man who claimed that a spirit attempted to kill him was experiencing his own self-hate. The young man who received word that he would kill his fiancée was receiving a message from the subconscious ambivalence he felt for her.

The other explanation is that these phenomena are produced by mischievous or evil spirits that have "possessed" these people. It is interesting that some parapsychologists support this opinion which is so similar to the conviction of those who say all parapsychology is the work of the devil. Of course, the parapsychologists go on to say that one should not condemn all parapsychology, even all mediumship or occult practices, just because a few of them turn out to harm some people. One does not condemn driving an automobile because some people are injured in accidents. What one does is warn people and help them so that they do not get into difficulty.

I personally do not discount the idea that some "evil" force may operate to cause frightening psychic phenomena, but I do feel that frequently these messages and urges that cause trouble are from a person's own subconscious mind. I believe this because in my opinion most ouija messages come through the subconscious influence of one's mind on the planchette.

I cannot personally believe that all or even a major portion of parapsychology is the work of the devil. I recognize the perils associated with certain practices, but I also see a great deal of good associated with many of them. The experimental work in parapsychology should be encouraged so that through this we may learn more about ourselves, our world, and the forces around us. The religious practices of prayer and healing have proved to be very valuable for many people. Even the occult practices, where most of the controversy is concentrated, may be beneficial and helpful for many people. It is not easy to draw a line between certain religious practices that some people attribute to the Holy Spirit and other occult practices that some people assign to the devil.

For example, I have heard some people condemn Jeane Dixon, who possesses the ability to foretell the future, as an instrument of the devil. But how can one draw a line between her work and that of Agabus, reported in Acts 11:28, who, under the power of the Spirit, foretold that there would be a great famine all over the world? The only possible test is, Do these predictions come true? Allen Spraggett, in his excellent book on Kathryn Kuhlman, reports that frequently in her services she is in an altered state of consciousness. She seems to go into a light trance in which she continues to function but seems somewhat unaware of what she is saying and doing. In this trancelike state, she receives clairvoyantly the information about people who are being healed. There is some indication, Mr. Spraggett reports, that on occasion Miss Kuhlman goes into an even deeper trance.[4] Can a person draw a line between Miss Kuhlman's trance, the trancelike state of a mystic, or the trancelike condition of a person speaking in tongues, and the trance of a medium? It seems to me that the same mechanism that operates in the trancelike state that people attribute to the Holy Spirit occurs also in the trance of a medium. The only way, then, to distinguish good and evil is to do so on the basis of what is produced. I have heard of situations in which what is called the baptism of the Holy Spirit had evil results, just as I have heard of situations in which visiting a medium had had good results. I cannot draw the line that consigns everything that people associate with the name of the Holy Spirit to the Kingdom of God, and everything associated with mediums to the realm of the devil. One must look at the results and ask if they are good or evil.

There is another reason I cannot draw that line. Perhaps I can illustrate this by describing a woman I know. In my opinion she is a sincere Christian, devoted to Christ and to his church. She possesses the gift of healing. She also professes to be able to see persons who have died and to receive messages from them. I personally cannot draw a line that splits her into two parts, one part controlled by the Holy Spirit when she heals and the other part controlled by the devil when she perceives the world of "spirits."

Saying that parapsychology or even a part of parapsychology is evil is a simplistic answer to a complex problem; it just doesn't fit all the situations. There are perils connected with some practices in this field, and I have tried to warn of these. However, there is much good to be gained from this field of endeavor too.

"Psychic phenomena prove that traditional Christian beliefs are true."

On the opposite end of the spectrum from those who say that psychic phenomena are the instruments of the devil are those who declare that psychic phenomena confirm traditional Christian beliefs. People who express this conviction usually begin their argument by saying that many Biblical events appear to be psychic phenomena. In the Bible are precognitive dreams such as those Joseph had; there are visions received in a trancelike state, such as Peter's vision, in which God declared that there are no unclean animals (Acts 10:9-16); there are healing miracles, which play so prominent a role in Jesus' ministry; there is communication from the dead— Jesus' conversation with Moses and Elijah on the Mount of Transfiguration; there is levitation—Jesus walking on the water; and there are out-of-body experiences such as the one reported by Paul in II Cor. 12:1-4. Even the resurrection itself some people view as a psychic event. The hurried conclusion to which some people leap is that God works in psychic events in this era just as he did in the Biblical era. What happened then has its counterpart now. So the fact that psychic events occur today proves that the Biblical record is true and confirms the truth of Christian faith.

On the surface this argument looks good, but there are some submerged rocks that can wreck this conviction. The first is that psychic events are not peculiar to Christianity. They can explain the origins of other great religions and of some of the Christian sect movements. So this conclusion imperils the belief that the Christian religion is unique.

But more serious than this is the fact that this conviction can lead to the conclusion that religion is a natural and not a supernatural phenomenon. All through this book I have tried to indicate that ESP, prayer, healing, and even survival may be natural events; that is, they may be the result of as yet undiscovered physical forces that operate in nature. If this is what proves to be true, when conclusive information becomes available, it could lead to the conclusion that psychic events that are described Biblically as supernatural events really are natural, and what we recognize as "God" is simply a force in nature. Such a conclusion threatens the traditional view of Christian faith and the structure of Christian beliefs. However, at the same time it does tend to affirm religious experience. One can hardly use psychic phenomena to support Christian dogma. One cannot even use them to confirm the traditional view of God. However, it does seem to me that one can say that psychic phenomena contribute to our understanding of religious experience. This is not to say that all psychic events are religious. It is to say that at certain points the two touch, and a fuller understanding of the one can contribute to a fuller understanding of the other.

"Whether or not psychic phenomena are real is not important to me. They will not affect the way I live."

Several weeks ago I learned through the news media that an astronomer had discovered that our solar system is passing through a cloud of hydrogen atoms which is at least fifty billion miles across. This information will have no effect on the way I live. Nevertheless, this discovery is interesting. This information adds to my general knowledge, and it is possible that it may be useful at some future time in understanding what is happening in our universe.

An understanding of psychic phenomena, though it may not necessarily affect the way a person lives, does help him to understand some of the experiences people have. As a pastor I have been asked on occasion about psychic events. A woman whose husband had died saw his form in the doorway. What did I think about that? A man revealed a strange phenomenon that accompanied his daughter's death. What did I think? A woman had the strong impression that her mother was in danger. What would I advise her to do? This is not an everyday experience, but it has occurred sufficiently often for me to try to understand such events more fully.

My personal view is that parapsychology is one of the new frontiers of human knowledge. I believe that as we learn more about psychic phenomena, we shall discover more about human thought and life. This knowledge will help us to improve the quality of life.

Furthermore, I am convinced that psychic events have a relationship with religious experience. I am not ready to define that relationship in precise form, largely because so much of the information about these events is as yet so imprecise. I feel, however, that the church particularly should pay close attention to what is happening in parapsychology. Religious experience, I am convinced, has a psychic dimension, and if we are to handle this area of life, we must keep current on the advances made in understanding it.

Psychic phenomena and religious experience are not synonymous terms. Religion is not a search for facts about life but for a faith that makes life meaningful. Facts cannot prove the faith affirmation, "Jesus Christ is Lord." Parapsychology will not produce the conviction, "I believe in God, the Father Almighty." The work of trance-mediums cannot prove the statement, "I believe in the resurrection of the body and the life everlasting." These affirmations and others like them are affirmations of faith, not fact. But the facts and theories related to parapsychology aid in our understanding of religious phenomena, and they help some people to see that their leap of faith is credible.

NOTES

Chapter 2. Extrasensory Perception

1. Louisa E. Rhine, *Hidden Channels of the Mind* (William Sloane Associates, Inc., 1961).

2. Louisa E. Rhine, *ESP in Life and Lab: Tracing Hidden Channels* (The Macmillan Company, 1967).

3. *Ibid.*, pp. 100-101.

4. *Ibid.*, pp. 162 ff.

5. Gordon E. W. Wolstenholme and Elaine C. P. Millar (eds.), *Extrasensory Perception* (Little, Brown and Company, 1956), pp. 53-72.

6. Joseph B. Rhine, *Extra-sensory Perception* (Bruce Humphries, Publishers, 1964).

7. *Ibid.*, p. 57.

8. *Ibid.*

9. *Ibid.*, pp. 81-82.

10. *Ibid.*, p. 90.

11. *Ibid.*, p. 98.

12. *Ibid.*, p. 114.

13. *Ibid.*, p. 139.

14. *Ibid.*, pp. 212-215.

15. *Ibid.*, p. 85.

16. *Ibid.*, p. 107.

17. *Ibid.*, p. 106.

18. *Ibid.*, pp. 201-202.

19. *Ibid.*, p. 176.

20. J. G. Pratt and J. L. Woodruff, "Size of Stimulus Symbols in Extra-sensory Perception," *International Journal of Parapsychology*, Vol. III (1939), pp. 121-158.

21. J. B. Rhine, *Extra-sensory Perception*, p. XXXV.

22. Samuel G. Soal and Frederick Bateman, *Modern Experiments in Telepathy* (Yale University Press, 1954), p. 151.

23. *Ibid.*, p. 226.

24. *Ibid.*, p. 244.

25. *Ibid.*, p. 292.

26. Samuel G. Soal and H. T. Bowden, *The Mind Readers* (Doubleday & Company, Inc., 1959), p. 237.

27. *Ibid.*, p. 264.

28. *Ibid.*, p. 104.

29. *Ibid.*, pp. 69, 76, 77.

30. *Ibid.*, pp. 87-88.

31. *Ibid.*, pp. 176-181.

32. C. E. M. Hansel, *ESP: A Scientific Evaluation* (Charles Scribner's Sons, 1966).

33. *Ibid.*, p. 76.

34. *Ibid.*, pp. 114-115.

35. *Ibid.*, p. 126.

36. *Ibid.*, p. 148.

37. *Ibid.*, p. 241.

38. Soal and Bowden, *The Mind Readers*, pp. 34-35.

39. L. E. Rhine, *ESP in Life and Lab*, pp. 169-170.

40. Joseph B. Rhine, *New World of the Mind* (William Sloane Associates, Inc., 1953), pp. 52-53.

41. L. E. Rhine, *ESP in Life and Lab*, p. 84.

42. *Ibid.*, pp. 83-90.

43. J. B. Rhine, *New World of the Mind*, p. 94.

44. E. Douglas Dean, "Non-Conventional Communication," *Proceedings of the First Space Congress* (Canaveral Council of Technical Societies, April 20-23, 1964), pp. 40-46.

45. John Mihalasky and E. Douglas Dean, "Bio-Communication" (presented at the Purdue Centennial Year Symposium on Information Processing, April 30, 1969, Purdue University, Lafayette, Indiana), p. 5.

46. *Ibid.*, p. 7.

47. *Ibid.*, p. 6.

48. L. E. Rhine, *ESP in Life and Lab*, pp. 229-230.

49. Gardner Murphy, *Challenge of Psychical Research* (Harper & Brothers, 1961), p. 115.

50. Gertrude R. Schmeidler and R. A. McConnell, *ESP and Personality Patterns* (Yale University Press, 1958), p. 33.

51. *Ibid.*, p. 53.

52. John Mihalasky, "Computer Scored Precognition Experiments" (paper presented at 11th Annual Convention Parapsychological Association, Freiburg, Germany, Sept. 5-7, 1968), p. 10.

53. J. Gaither Pratt, *Parapsychology: An Insider's View of ESP* (Doubleday & Company, Inc., 1964), pp. 207-209.

54. Cleve Backster, "Evidence of a Primary Perception in Plant Life," *International Journal of Parapsychology*, Vol. X, No. 4 (Winter, 1968), p. 330.

55. *Ibid.*, p. 345.

56. Thorn Bacon, "The Man Who Reads Nature's Secret Signals," *National Wildlife*, Feb.-March, 1969, p. 7.

57. Charles McCreery, *Science, Philosophy, and ESP* (London: Faber and Faber, 1967), p. 116.

58. *Ibid.*, p. 154.

59. T. D. Duane and Thomas Behrendt, "Extrasensory Electroencephalographic Induction Between Identical Twins," *Science*, Vol. 150 (Oct. 15, 1965), p. 367.

Chapter 3. Prayer

1. William R. Parker and Elaine St. Johns, *Prayer Can Change Your Life* (Prentice-Hall, Inc., 1957).

2. *Ibid.*, p. 34.

3. Franklin Loehr, *The Power of Prayer on Plants* (Doubleday & Company, Inc., 1959).

4. *Ibid.*, pp. 43-44.

5. *Ibid.*, p. 47.

6. *Ibid.*, p. 50.

7. *Ibid.*, p. 59.

8. *Ibid.*, p. 69.

9. *Ibid.*, p. 78.

10. *Ibid.*, pp. 90-91.

11. *Ibid.*, p. 88.

12. Evelyn Underhill, *Mysticism* (Meridian Books, Inc., 1955), p. 70.

13. William R. Inge, *Christian Mysticism* (Meridian Books, Inc., 1956), pp. 10-12.

14. D. T. Suzuki, *An Introduction to Zen Buddhism* (Grove Press, Inc., 1964), p. 44.

15. D. T. Suzuki, *Mysticism: Christian and Buddhist* (Harper & Brothers, 1957), p. 40.

16. John Mihalasky, "Computer Scored Precognition Experiments" (unpublished document), p. 9.

17. *Ibid.*

Chapter 4. Spiritual Healing

1. Bernard Martin, *The Healing Ministry of the Church* (John Knox Press, 1960), p. 19.

2. *Ibid.*, pp. 14-15.

3. *Ibid.*, p. 38.

4. Wade H. Boggs, Jr., *Faith Healing and the Christian Faith* (John Knox Press, 1956), pp. 68-69.

5. Kathryn Kuhlman, *I Believe in Miracles* (Prentice-Hall, Inc., 1962).

6. Allen Spraggett, *Kathryn Kuhlman: The Woman Who Believes in Miracles* (The World Publishing Company, 1970), p. 172.

7. Ambrose A. Worrall, with Olga N. Worrall, *The Gift of Healing* (Harper & Row, Publishers, Inc., 1965), p. 139.

8. *Ibid.*, pp. 142-151.

9. John Sutherland Bonnell, *Do You Want to Be Healed?* (Harper & Row, Publishers, Inc., 1968), p. 20.

10. *Ibid.*

11. *Ibid.*, p. 21.

12. *Ibid.*, p. 23.

13. Franz Alexander, *Psychosomatic Medicine* (W. W. Norton & Company, Inc., 1950), pp. 46-47.

14. Edward Weiss and O. Spurgeon English, *Psychosomatic Medicine* (W. B. Saunders Company, 1957), pp. 4-5.

15. B. Grad, R. J. Cadoret, and G. I. Paul, "The Influence of an Unorthodox Method of Treatment on Wound Healing in Mice," *International Journal of Parapsychology*, Vol. III, No. 2 (Spring, 1961), pp. 5-24.

16. *Ibid.*, pp. 14-16.

17. *Ibid.*, p. 17.

18. Bernard Grad, "A Telekinetic Effect on Plant Growth," *International Journal of Parapsychology*, Vol. V, No. 2 (Spring, 1963), pp. 117-133.

19. *Ibid.*, pp. 120-124.

20. *Ibid.*, p. 131.

21. Bernard Grad, "The 'Laying on of Hands': Implication for Psychotherapy, Gentling and the Placebo Effect," *Journal of the American Society for Psychical Research*, Vol. 61 (1967), pp. 286-305.

22. Jeanne Pontius Rindge, "Are There 'Healing Hands'?", Rosary Hill *Response*, Vol. II, No. 2 (Spring, 1968), p. 20.

23. *Ibid.*, pp. 21 and 31.

24. Spraggett, *Kathryn Kuhlman*, p. 146.

Chapter 5. Personal Survival

1. Arthur Ford, with Margueritte H. Bro, *Nothing So Strange* (Paperback Library, Inc., 1968), pp. 10-11.

2. Arthur Ford, *Unknown but Known: My Adventure Into the Meditative Dimension* (Harper & Row, Publishers, Inc., 1968), p. 58.

3. Hereward Carrington, *Mysterious Psychic Phenomena* (Christopher Publishing House, 1954), p. 142.

4. Samuel G. Soal and Frederick Bateman, *Modern Experiments in Telepathy* (Yale University Press, 1954), pp. 263-265.

5. James A. Pike, *The Other Side* (Dell Publishing Co., Inc., 1968), pp. 221-222.

6. *Ibid.*, pp. 277-278.

7. S. Ralph Harlow, *A Life After Death* (MacFadden-Bartell, Corp., 1968), pp. 60-62.

8. Gardner Murphy, *Three Papers on the Survival Problem* (The American Society for Psychical Research, Inc., 1945), p. 208.

9. *Ibid.*, pp. 22-23.

10. G. N. M. Tyrrell, *Apparitions* (Collier Books, 1963), p. 101.

11. *Ibid.*

12. *Ibid.*, pp. 85-88.

13. *Ibid.*, pp. 35-36.

14. Karlis Osis, *Deathbed Observations by Physicians and Nurses* (Parapsychology Foundation, Inc., 1961), p. 61.

15. *Ibid.*, p. 31.
16. Carrington, *Mysterious Psychic Phenomena*, p. 62.
17. Osis, *Deathbed Observations*, p. 64.
18. Tyrrell, *Apparitions*, pp. 45-46.
19. *Ibid.*, p. 111.
20. *Ibid.*, p. 112.
21. *Ibid.*, pp. 112-113.
22. C. J. Ducasse, *A Critical Examination of the Belief in a Life After Death* (Charles C. Thomas, Publishers, 1961), pp. 156-157.
23. Tyrrell, *Apparitions*, pp. 165-171.
24. Harold Sherman, *How to Make ESP Work for You* (Fawcett Publications, Inc., 1964), pp. 138-139.
25. Allen Spraggett, *The Unexplained* (The New American Library, Inc., 1967), p. 180.
26. Ducasse, *A Critical Examination*, p. 164.
27. Morey Bernstein, *The Search for Bridey Murphy* (Pocket Books, Inc., 1956).
28. Ducasse, *A Critical Examination*, pp. 279-295.
29. Ian Stevenson, *Twenty Cases Suggestive of Reincarnation* (American Society for Psychical Research, 1966), p. 89.
30. *Ibid.*, p. 109.
31. *Ibid.*, pp. 181 and 186.
32. *Ibid.*, p. 216.
33. *Ibid.*, p. 206.
34. *Ibid.*, pp. 216-217.
35. *Ibid.*, pp. 294-295.
36. *Ibid.*, p. 306.
37. *Ibid.*, p. 309.
38. *Ibid.*, p. 340.
39. *Ibid.*, p. 347.
40. *Ibid.*, p. 34.

Chapter 6. Psychic Phenomena and Religion

1. Louisa E. Rhine, *Mind Over Matter* (The Macmillan Company, 1970).
2. Jule Eisenbud, *The World of Ted Serios* (William Morrow and Company, Inc., 1967), pp. 257-262.
3. Hugh Lynn Cayce, *Venture Inward* (Paperback Library, Inc., 1964), pp. 130-141.
4. Spraggett, *Kathryn Kuhlman*, p. 125.